THE BIBLE AND THE
BERMUDA TRIANGLE

by George Johnson & Don Tanner

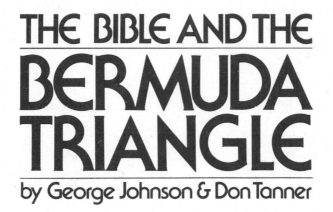

D0048541

Logos International
Plainfield, New Jersey

The Bible and the Bermuda Triangle
Copyright © 1976 by George Johnson and Don Tanner
Published by Logos International
All rights reserved
Printed in the United States of America
Library of Congress catalog card number: 76-45525
International Standard Book Number: 0-88270-209-2 (Trade softcover)
Logos International, Plainfield, New Jersey 07061

Publisher's Preface

The Bermuda Triangle is a name that evokes a sense of mystery, darkness and, sometimes, fear in the hearts of countless people. Why is that? George Johnson and Don Tanner think they have an answer. It is one they have derived largely from the Bible. Many will regard their hypothesis as bizarre or absurd, but many others will regard it as an intriguing possibility. We at Logos appreciate the tentative tone with which the authors advance their theory, which is part of the reason we decided to publish it.

Thus we present it, not as a doctrine that must be believed, but as something to think about.

Acknowledgments

To the congregants who have had faith in me for the past sixteen years, especially those who have prayed and supported the efforts of this book. To Tom, Richard, Marcelle, Ralph and Peggy whose investment in this book initiated its beginning. To Pat and Sue, who typed the manuscript and revisions. To my wife, Nancy, who had patience and understanding in the many hours of research and study and who in my absence had a real flood when a four-inch water main burst and flooded the church. To my God and Savior be the glory, for without His Spirit our eyes would still be in darkness.

George Johnson

To my wife, Sally, whose support of my ministry means everything, and who through self-giving love endured many hours of loneliness so I could share in writing and editing this book.

Don Tanner

TABLE OF CONTENTS

Introduction vii

Chapter 1
The Mystery of Inner Space 1

Chapter 2
The Lost Cities 29

Chapter 3
The Sargasso Sea 51

Chapter 4
The Devil's Triangle 61

Chapter 5
Mystery Solved 85

Chapter 6
Abyss under the Sea 97

Chapter 7
Leviathan—King of the Sea 117

Chapter 8
Abaddon—King of the Abyss 135

Chapter 9
Creatures of the Deep 143

Chapter 10
The End of the World 161

Appendixes
To Chapter 1 171

To Chapter 2 179

To Chapter 6 197

To Chapter 7 199

To Chapter 8 205

Introduction

In *The Bible and the Bermuda Triangle*, the unsolved legends of missing ships, planes and people are explained through the most ancient book of all—the Bible.

The co-authors are George Johnson, pastor of the Cathedral of Life Church, Torrance, California; and Don Tanner, religion editor of *The Daily Breeze*, Torrance, a major suburban daily newspaper in Los Angeles County.

Johnson's interest in the subject came after reading books on the Bermuda Triangle and a personal study of the Book of Revelation. A deeper study of Scripture and the Triangle phenomena led him to make startling discoveries of the similarities and correlations between the disruptions of the seas and strange disappearances and the location of the nether world.

Tanner's interest came through reading news accounts of the Bermuda Triangle and the reports of people who have been permitted to see and experience life beyond the grave and who returned to describe the places they have visited.

His interest has been to correlate these experiences with the biblical evidences that such experiences can occur and that life exists in worlds beyond the grave.

In this book the authors seek to prove the existence of Sheol-Hades and that it is located under the sea. They show that the catastrophic disturbances in parts of the world can be attributed to spiritual activity over the entrances to the nether world.

Universal upheavals in the world, including Lucifer's flood and Noah's flood, and the lost continent Atlantis—did it exist and what is its significance?—are examined.

The nether world (Sheol-Hades) is defined as "a place of inquiry" where man's curiosity arouses his interest. If it does exist—as the abode of the departed—then the alternative is redemption through the cross of Christ.

The authors also give physical descriptions of Sheol-Hades and its residents and discuss the significance of such nether world beings as Abaddon, king of destruction; and Leviathan, king of pride.

The book ends on a positive note. It tells where the redeemed go after death and shows the significance of water in the kingdom of God in contrast to its present role as a destructive and captive force.

Chapter 1

The Mystery of Inner Space

The secret things belong to the LORD our God, but the things revealed belong to us and to our sons forever, that we may observe all the words of this law (Deut. 29:29).

Why do compasses point only true north in the Bermuda Triangle and in the Devil's Sea off the coast of Japan?

Why do eels migrate to the depths of the Triangle?

Why does seaweed of the Sargasso Sea only exist in the area of the Triangle (growing on the surface of the sea while the ocean floor is eighteen thousand feet below)?

Why are hurricanes spawned in the Bermuda Triangle?

Why do clairvoyants such as Edgar Cayce and M.B. Dykshoorn say there is no mystery to the Triangle?

The mysteries of inner space and their effects on the world above have long baffled mariners and experts in related fields.

But the Bible, the most ancient book of all, has much to say about these mysteries, about the ancient past and the prophetic future. In this book, we will look at its pages to find the things revealed about the mysteries and their significance for man.

Secrets of the Past

The sea is a key to man's past.

Evolutionists say life evolved from it.

Occultists trace their origins to lost continents which they say lie beneath it.

Geologists have attempted to bore through Earth's crust under the sea to find clues to the age and composition of our planet.

And zoologists recently have been startled to find living specimens of supposedly extinct species, known previously only by fossil remains. Several living segmented mollusks [1] have been dredged from a depth of 11,700 feet in the Acapulco Trench off Central America; these mollusks supposedly became extinct about 280 million years ago! Living coelecanths and crustaceans also have been found, which again were supposed to be extinct some 70 to 300 million years ago.[2]

In the near future what other "index fossils" will the ocean's depths expose, and what other secrets to man's past will be found beneath the sea?

The Bermuda Triangle has claimed more than a thousand lives in the past twenty-five years as planes and ships have vanished, leaving no trace of bodies or wreckage. One hundred planes and ships have vanished in the Triangle, most of them since 1945, and according to many recent books, mysterious disappearances are continuing to occur despite modern technology's ability to track and find lost craft.

2

The *Nereus*-sister ship to the U.S.S. *Cyclops*-is seen here some time after 1913. The ship left the Virgin Islands on December 10, 1941, headed for Portland, Maine, and disappeared without a trace while en route. Photo: U.S. Navy.

What secrets does the sea in the Triangle hold concerning these disappearances?

What happened to Flight 19, the five Navy TBM Avengers that disappeared during a routine training mission from Fort Lauderdale Naval Air Station on December 5, 1945? They were the object of one of the most intensive ground-sea rescue operations ever conducted. No life rafts, oil slicks or wreckage were ever located, and the Martin Mariner aircraft sent to rescue them also disappeared— without a trace.

Other aircraft, including passenger planes, have vanished while receiving landing instructions—almost as if they had flown through a hole in the sky, according to the Naval Board of Inquiry.

Large ships, such as the 19,000-ton USS *Cyclops* with 309 people aboard, have vanished while other ships and boats have been found drifting in the Triangle with only a dog or canary aboard as sole survivors.

Col. Harvey Wolfe, an authority on unsolved mysteries, says, "Normally when an aircraft goes down there will be some evidence left behind of how it met its fate. Not so with the more than 1,000 ships, aircraft and small boats that have disappeared from the area known as the Bermuda Triangle.

"Even shark fishermen have been questioned. Sometimes when a ship is lost, part of a person is found in a shark. But the sharks in the Triangle haven't provided any clues to the unusual disappearances.

"An American airplane flying from Puerto Rico to Miami was only 50 miles away from its destination when the pilot asked for landing instructions. The instructions were given and acknowledged and the airplane, its crew and passengers disappeared, never to be heard from again.

"I was involved in the search for that plane," Wolfe says. "It was frustrating. There was nothing, no oil slick, no life jackets, nothing, just blank ocean.

"There has been a constant loss of ships, yachts and people, but no one knows the answer, and there's not been one bit of wreckage found." [3]

Wayne Meshejian, an assistant professor of physics at Longwood College, Farmville, Virginia, has studied another phenomenon in the Triangle. For the past three-and-a-half years Meshejian and his students have monitored four weather satellites launched by the National Oceanographic and Atmospheric Administration (NOAA). Two— NOAA-3 and NOAA-4—are still aloft.

"Three of the satellites we've monitored all have the same features; they send down both infrared and visible pictures of the Earth's weather patterns. But they are unable to send both down at once. Instead, they send a piece of infrared, then visible, then infrared and so forth. In order to delay the visible picture while the infrared is being sent down, it is temporarily stored on a magnetic loop in the satellite," Meshejian says.

"The machine records, then erases, records, erases. As best I can tell, when the satellite goes over the Bermuda Triangle area, something apparently is causing the visible picture to black out.

"I assume that whatever is doing this is causing the tape recorder to malfunction. This would mean we have something of a magnetic nature interfering with the tape."

Controversy has developed since he delivered a lecture on his findings.

"I called a gentleman with NOAA," he says. "He told me the government was responsible for this blackout. If this is so, then the government has a good deal of explaining to do. In years past, if anything went wrong with satellites, even a slight electrical malfunction, they were very prompt to contact all the people who worked on it. I have seen satellites black out when they go over the Triangle, and when it comes back around the world, it's still blacked out." [4]

What other mysteries does the sea hold?

Natural Triangle Phenomena

PUERTO RICO TRENCH—The deepest cataracts in the Atlantic Ocean run along the north and south of the Antilles, which comprise the islands of Cuba, Haiti, Dominican Republic and Puerto Rico.

Off San Juan, the southern tip of the Triangle, the depths fall to 27,500 feet under the sea, and if one was to bore a hole straight through the Earth parallel with the equator, he would come within two hundred miles of the Mariana

Trench, the deepest gorge in the Pacific Ocean's depths, about thirty-six thousand feet deep off the island of Guam.

Recent books on the Triangle state that many ships and planes strangely have disappeared in the Triangle's counterpart on the opposite side of the world, the Devil's Sea, ranging roughly from Guam to the Philippines to Japan.

At the bottom of the Sargasso Sea are the Hatteras and Nares Abyssal Plains. These flat beds of sedimentation lie at depths of nineteen thousand feet.

Charles Berlitz says the ocean bottom under the Bermuda Triangle was formed some ten to twelve thousand years ago. "In 1956 Drs. R. Malaise and P. Kolbe of the National Museum of Stockholm offered the opinion that skeletons of fresh-water diatoms, which Dr. Kolbe had brought up in a sample core from a depth of 12,000 feet near the Atlantic Ridge, had originally been deposited in a fresh-water lake, formerly on the surface of land now sunk to the bottom of the ocean," Berlitz says. "These fresh-water diatoms were estimated at 10,000 to 12,000 years." [5]

Berlitz says there is strong evidence that a continental land mass existed in the Caribbean Sea, and the islands and ridges of the Antilles may be the surviving mountain peaks.

"In 1969 a research expedition from Duke University studied the sea bottom of the Caribbean and conducted dredging operations at a number of places on the Aves Ridge," he says. "On fifty occasions granitic (acid igneous) rocks were brought to the surface. A distinguished oceanographer, Dr. Bruce Heezen, in commenting on this matter, has observed: 'Up to now, geologists generally believed that light granitic, or acid igneous rocks, are confined to the continents and that the crust of the earth beneath the sea is composed of heavier, dark-colored basaltic rock. . . . Thus, the occurrence of light-colored granitic rocks may support an old theory that a continent formerly existed in the region

The Sargasso Sea, where legends of lost ships have abounded since the time of Columbus. Photo: Courtesy, The Mariners Museum, Newport News, Va.

of the eastern Caribbean and that these rocks may represent the core of a subsided, lost continent.' " [6]

What caused the collapse of the ocean floor? Was this an ancient continent that had a sudden cataclysmic upheaval?

SARGASSO SEA—This is a Portuguese word for several species of gulfweed, *sargaco*, L. *sargassum*.

It also is the name of a zone in the southwest region of the North Atlantic, just south of the main arm of the Gulf Stream. These island-like masses cover an area of 1.5 million square miles or eight times the area of France. They form off the coast of Florida and are carried to the Sargasso Sea by the swirling currents of the Gulf Stream. This residue accumulates over the Bermuda Triangle, almost like debris that has surfaced from sunken remains.

Columbus' sailors felt great fear when they saw "the

tropical grapes" and believed they were close to land and sailing in shallow waters. Actually at that point they were twenty-two thousand feet above the ocean floor.

The Gulf Stream flows on the west of this stagnant area; the Canary and North Equatorial streams flow on the east and the south. This leaves almost a deadly calm, which probably gave rise to the unnerving legend of the "sea of lost ships" and "sea of fear."

There are legends dating back to 500 B.C. concerning the mariners who crossed the Sargasso Sea. One such legend by the Carthaginian Admiral Himilco is as follows:

> . . . No breeze drives the ship, so dead is the sluggish wind of the idle sea . . . there is much seaweed among the waves, it holds back the ship like bushes. . . .

Here is a definite chord of seaweed fields and the lack of wind. Even the name *horse latitude,* which runs directly through the Triangle and Sargasso Sea, is an indication of the stagnant calm; when the Spanish galleons were stalled for lack of wind, the Spaniards reluctantly were forced to kill their war horses to save water.

Sailor legends also warned mariners before Columbus that there was a great Atlantic surface graveyard containing ships of all ages of seafaring man:

> If a ship were becalmed long enough to use up her stores, she would eventually grow grass and barnacles until she became virtually unable to sail. And that tropical borer worms would bore into the sides of the vessel until a rotted and putrid mess, manned by skeletons . . . slipped below the heated surface of the calm sea.[7]

Abandoned Vessels—found floating at sea, like this ship, with no life aboard (February, 1940) characterize the story of the Bermuda Triangle. Photo: United Press International.

SPAWNING OF EELS—European and American eels spawn in the Bermuda Triangle.

Aristotle (384-322 B.C.) was the first naturalist of antiquity reported to have brought up the puzzling question concerning the breeding grounds of European eels. The eels were known to leave their ponds, lakes, streams and small rivers and swim down the large rivers that empty in the sea. Dr. Johannes Schmidt, a Danish scientist, twenty-five hundred years later discovered where the eels have been going.

The adult European eels follow the waterways that empty into the Atlantic; there they unite and swim in a great shoal, progressing slowly for about four months. They are accompanied by flights of feeding gulls and packs of sharks until they reach the point in the Sargasso Sea where they spawn at a considerable depth. There the adults die, and the

9

newly born eels (called leptocephali) start their long trip back to Europe, borne by the Gulf Stream, a trip which takes about two years.

Eels from the American continent follow the same patterns in reverse. These eels swim eastward and meet the European eels in the depths of the Sargasso Sea, and the young eels return to their ancestral homes in America. One theory concerning this is that eels still seek out their original spawning grounds at the site of the vanished river, which once flowed through a continent now thousands of feet under the sea.

What connection could these serpentine creatures and the Sargasso Sea have in the Triangle? The Sargasso Sea and the eels have no counterpart anywhere in the world.

MAGNETIC FIELDS—Why do compasses only point true north in the Bermuda Triangle and its counterpart the Devil's Sea off the coast of Japan?

Erratic compasses are a characteristic phenomenon troubling those lost at sea.

Warren and Betty Miller of East Lansing, Michigan, know about this first hand. They have flown the mysterious Triangle many times in their twin-engine Beechcraft E-95.

The Millers were on their way back to the United States from Guatemala when the plane's dials stopped functioning.

"We still can't explain what happened," Mrs. Miller says. "Every other time we've left our refueling stop at Cozumel we would see the Honduras coast for at least 20 minutes.

"Then after you can't see Honduras, you come in sight of Cuba. But all the time we were out there we had no sight of the island.

"All we could see was a yellowish haze. My husband made a 30-degree turn, which we thought should have put us over Cuba, but still there was only the yellow haze.

Waterspout—These sea-going tornadoes can rip apart a ship or plane, if their paths were to cross. Photo: World Wide Photos

"At first we thought it was the island or the shadow of a cloud down there on the ocean. I can't explain it. It was very eerie. There wasn't anything there."

They were flying at eleven thousand feet with a dead instrument panel.

After many tries, the couple managed to pick up Havana on their shortwave and shortly afterward a signal from Florida, which guided them to Key West.

"They say it wasn't the instruments, and I don't know what else it could have been," Miller says, "Except maybe the area. The instruments never acted up before, and they haven't acted up since we left the Devil's Triangle" (another name for the Bermuda Triangle).

Mrs. Miller has some theories about the Triangle. "I've never seen a UFO or anything, but I know that something is out there that pulls and does something to instruments." [8]

What magnetic force causes this?

In all other parts of the world compasses point to magnetic north, and the difference between the two is known as compass variation. The amount of variation changes as much as twenty degrees as one circumnavigates the Earth.

Physical Disturbances

HURRICANES AND TYPHOONS—called hurricanes in the Bermuda Triangle and typhoons in the Devil's Sea.

These destructive wind forces create havoc every year to the islands and countries in their paths. The cold north currents coming in contact with the warmer equatorial streams create devastating wind forces. These cyclonic storms reach winds up to one hundred and fifty miles an hour.

Banner I. Miller in "Characteristics of Hurricanes" (*Science*, Sept. 22, 1967, p. 1397) says meteorologists know less about the formation of hurricanes than about their existence.

The disturbances from which hurricanes grow occur almost daily somewhere over the tropical oceans, yet few develop into full-grown hurricanes.

The formation of a hurricane is a relatively rare event, and scientists do not yet understand all the links in the chain which cause these events to occur.

This raises the question behind the reasons why these destructive forces are so prevalent over these two areas.

Could there be more than the mixing of the hot and cold currents?

WATERSPOUTS—Seagoing tornadoes, which occur at certain seasons and raise vast funnels of water to great heights in the sky.

A waterspout can tear apart a boat or a low-flying plane in the same way that a tornado on land tears apart or carries houses, fences, vehicles and people into the sky.

Captain Joshua Slocum was the world's best-known sailor of his day. He was the first man in history known to have sailed around the world single-handedly. He is seen here near Washington, D.C., in May, 1907. Two years later, he set sail from Martha's Vineyard, bound for South America. He was never seen again. Photo: Courtesy, The Mariners Museum, Newport News, Va.

Waterspouts can be seen during the day, and there is enough time to take evasive action. But not at night. Then ships and planes are at their mercy. Again, it is in these areas that many of them are spawned. Could there be a connection between their destructive forces and mystery forces under the sea?

CLEAR AIR TURBULENCE—Stresses exist in the atmosphere that can be roughly compared with tidal waves. The turbulence (CAT) may go up or down or in different horizontal directions. When planes encounter CAT the effect is almost like flying into a brick wall.

Berlitz says, "Generally speaking, CAT cannot be predicted, although it is generally encountered at the edge of a jet stream, the air current that moves through the skies above the Earth much as the Gulf Stream moves through the ocean, but with considerably more speed—200 knots per hour as compared with the Gulf Stream's four knots or less. CAT could possibly explain the loss of some of the light planes in the Bermuda Triangle, tearing them apart according to the amount of pressure exerted (the G factor) or suddenly forming a vacuum and dropping the plane into the sea. . . . Nevertheless, it is doubtful that sudden pressure change could have been the reason for all of the many planes lost in the Triangle and could have knocked out their radio communications as well." [9]

TSUNAMIS—These huge waves are caused by earthquake disturbances. They have been known to reach a height of two hundred feet. The giant waves can come without warning and can easily sink a ship. Not only do small ships sink, but larger ones have been known to break in half from the tension.

The USS *Ramapo* on February 6, 1963 reported one wave 112 feet high.

Underwater landslides can cause huge waves (seiche).

The *Spray* was Joshua Slocum's boat, on which he sailed into oblivion in November, 1909. Photo: Courtesy, The Mariners Museum, Newport News, Va.

These are caused by the pulling apart of a fault in the Earth's crust. These waves, though smaller in height, are more deceptive. They have great amounts of powerful tides of water built up behind them. Such a wave could smash a ship and leave its wreckage strewn over long distances, losing parts of it as it travels.

Could these sudden waves be the cause of some of the disappearances?

The Ancient Past

PLATO'S ATLANTIC ACCOUNT—The mystery surrounding the Bermuda Triangle is ancient and legendary. Plato told of a lost continent in the Atlantic four hundred years before Christ.

His account came from an earlier one written by Solon, an Athenian statesman, which describes a conversation between Egyptian priests and Solon on one of his frequent visits to Egypt.

The wise men of Sais reported it to Solon, but because of the length of the work it was never finished. It then was left to Plato to finish the story at a later date.

His account begins by saying that the gods divided the Earth between themselves and built temples for sacrifices. Poseidon, the Greek god of the seas, married a mortal woman and settled on the island of Atlantis. His wife, Cleito, bore him five sets of twins, all boys, and he made them rulers over ten portions of the island. He gave them all names, from Atlas, his oldest son, to Diaprepes his youngest. The Atlantic was named after Atlas.

The temple was dedicated to Poseidon and Cleito and was surrounded with an enclosure of gold. The animals that they sacrificed were horses. The description of his kingdom was one of "rare metals, wood, tame and wild animals, elephants, harbors, canals, central royal palace, stones

16

UFO Tails Army Copter—In January, 1976, Major Claude Riddle, pictured here, spotted a UFO on the tail of his helicopter. A veteran pilot, he described it as "shimmering like a diamond and as big as a jet-liner." Twenty-four other people also sighted the same object. Photo: Reprinted by permission of the NATIONAL ENQUIRER.

which were quarried (cf. Ezek. 28) and Poseidon's temple—with springs and trees."

In short, Atlantis was a "garden of Eden," a paradise. Plato goes on to say that as long as the *divine nature* lasted in them and they were obedient to the laws and loved the gods, everything was alright. But when the *divine portion* began to fade in them, *human nature* got the upper hand, and they began to appear base. It was at this time that Zeus, god of gods who rules with law, called a conference with his gods. The account abruptly ends here.

In this unfinished *Critias*, Atlantas is a utopia of a former civilization. In the *Timaeus*, he describes the destruction of Atlantis "in a day and a night" by a great cataclysmic deluge. This sudden upheaval filled the sea with mud and interfered with navigation.

OTHER HISTORIANS—The next historians who mentioned Atlantis include Crantor (300 B.C.) who believed the story to be true. Poseidonius (135-51 B.C.), a Stoic philosopher and writer who traveled widely, believed the Atlantis story was a combination of actual and imaginary events. Strabo (67 B.C.-A.D. 23), the great geographer of antiquity, held the same view while the Alexandrine scholars (A.D. 330-400) believed the destruction of Atlantis to be an historical fact.

Nevertheless, the great impetus for fresh speculations on the Atlantis mystery was provided by Christopher Columbus' explorations in the Caribbean. In 1553 Francesco Lopez de Gomara theorized that America was the continent on the other side of the Atlantic referred to in the Platonic dialogues. Later, Sir Francis Bacon put forward the hypothesis that the newly discovered continent was in fact Atlantis.

It wasn't until 1882 when a former United States Congressman from Minnesota wrote his Atlantic classic, *Atlantis: the Antediluvian World*, that a resurgence of interest in the subject began. Although there are more than five thousand works on Atlantis, its popularity has grown since Ignatius Donnelly's new scientific deductions.

Ties with the Occult

Ivan Sanderson, late scientist and advocate of the lost continent Atlantis, suggests, in *Invisible Residents*, that ". . . there is an underwater civilization on this planet that has been here for a very long time . . ." and that it is considerably more advanced than ours.

Berlitz says such a subterranean civilization in the Triangle would explain why numerous reliable observers have seen UFOs under clear waters and in the skies—going from the sea to the sky and from the sky to the sea.[10]

Dr. Manson Valentine, an oceanographer who has studied the unusual happenings of the Triangle for several decades from the Triangle itself, notes:

> UFOs in the sky have been seen so often in the Triangle by pilots of aircraft and crews of ships that they have become fairly commonplace, especially over the Tongue of the Ocean.

He assumed there are intelligent beings directing the UFOs who are "not only taking samples and checking our scientific progress . . . but are returning to what may have been the location of ancient sacred sites, perhaps energy centers or power stations that are now covered by the sea. We have in recent years discovered, near Bimini and other places in the Bahamas, great building complexes on the sea bottom, an indication that a high state of civilization existed here many thousands of years ago. It is more than curious that so many incidents happen in this area and so many UFOs are seen not only in the sky but entering and leaving the ocean." [12]

UFO sightings in the Triangle are more frequent than elsewhere in the world, giving rise to speculations that UFOs are hauling planes and ships, with their crews and passengers, off to another world.

John Spencer, author of *Limbo of the Lost,* supports the UFO hijacking theory:

> Since the complete disappearance of 575-foot vessels in calm seas 50 miles offshore or commercial airlines going in for a landing cannot happen ac-

cording to earthly standards and yet are happening, I am forced to conclude that they are being taken away from our planet.[13]

One of the unusual elements of the mysterious disappearance of Flight 19 in 1945 is the possibility of UFO involvement. It was reported twenty-nine years later by author and lecturer Art Ford. He made the startling revelation in 1974 over a national television program that flight leader Lt. Charles Taylor said over his radio during an emergency message to the tower, "Don't come after me . . . they look like they are from outer space."

Ford said the conversation was heard by a ham-radio operator, but he didn't give much credence to it until years later when he spotted the phrase "Don't come after me" while examining a formerly secret transcript of the flight leader's transmissions.

"This final mystery," Berlitz says, "with its suggestion of other-world interference, is echoed in more than a few of the other disappearances." [14]

Berlitz' reference to "other-world interference" is interesting. There is overwhelming biblical evidence of a spiritual and supernatural world that is not perceptible to our senses, yet it moves parallel to our material existence and affects us profoundly. The parallel world is the abode of spirits.

John Weldon, in *UFOs: What on Earth is Happening?*, discusses this parallel world in conjunction with UFOs.

The parallel world . . . is a very full world, occupied by a variety of beings and entities, rather like the world we see. The Bible characterizes the spiritual world as experiencing ongoing warfare on the angelic level—the very sons of God are in contention. We see it clearly in the painful experiences of Job, and we will see it objectively revealed in the Tribulation to come.

The Book of Revelation presents quite a different world from that which we are accustomed to: in the end times of Revelation, the spiritual beings of good and evil will make themselves manifest on the Earth, and there will be no further doubt as to what sort of conflict has been going on in their Province.[15]

The spirit world is tremendously significant to the material world. As Weldon says:

Essential matters vital to us all and yet not definable by natural or scientific means, like love, beauty, God, evil, ESP, and most likely UFOs, are all around us. We are aware of them only through their intrusion into our affairs, not by observations.[16]

We believe entities in the parallel world are intruding into the material realm, and we are seeing the effects in a world rapidly moving toward a period of tremendous geological, social, political and religious upheaval.

While we know the means of their information is rooted in the occult, it is significant that psychics everywhere are predicting a great upheaval of Earth before the year two thousand. Judging from Bible prophecies and world conditions, there seems to be an element of truth in their timing.

While geological cataclysm appears on the horizon, there is another upheaval going on that is even more significant. It is the climate of humanity.

The powers of darkness are concentrating their efforts

on our moorless society. Just as intense evil precipitated God's judgment of Earth in the Noahic Flood, so evil is dragging today's world toward disaster.

Evil is manifesting itself not only in sins common to man since the fall of Adam, but in a dramatic revival of occultism and Satan worship.

As Weldon says:

Some theologians credit demons, like the ones mentioned throughout Scripture, with the periodic global manifestation of evil which have plagued our world. [17]

Lewis Chafer says, "A similar increase in the activity of demons is predicted for the close of this age and in the Great Tribulation." [18]

We agree with Weldon that demons—spirit beings from the parallel world—are behind the UFO phenomenon. (See appendix.)

The fact that UFOs are included in the mysteries of the Triangle brings another dimension to what is happening there.

While a great percentage of the disappearances and other phenomena of the Triangle can be attributed to natural causes, there is enough of the mysterious and unexplainable to arouse questions that must be answered. Whether explainable or not, it is our thesis that entities from the parallel world are involved. Something doesn't have to be mysterious or unexplainable to be influenced by the spirit world. What may appear supernatural to us is very natural to that world. And the influence of that world is strong upon ours.

Jesus, while in His earthly body, for example, spoke to the wind and the sea, and they obeyed Him (Matt. 8:27; 14:24-32; Mark 4:39); God parted the Red Sea for Moses "by a strong east wind" (Exod. 14:21); and angels can prevent the wind from blowing (Rev. 7:1) or cause an earthquake (Matt. 28:2).

Evil entities have powers similar to good beings, but use them for destructive means. Satan, the Bible says, can pose as an angel of light with intellectual knowledge, positive ideas and appealing philosophies; but his intent is delusion, entrapment and destruction.

There is sufficient evidence in Scripture to say that God often uses evil emissaries to bring judgment or trial.

Job, for example.

On one occasion, fire came from the sky and burned up his shepherds and sheep, and a "great wind from the wilderness"—possibly a tornado—destroyed a son's house, killing everyone in it. We know Satan was behind these incidents because God said to Satan, ". . . all that he (Job) has is in your power. . . . So Satan departed from the presence of the Lord" and bad things began to happen to Job (Job 1:12-22).

Diabolical entities are behind much of the physical disturbances in the Triangle, as we'll see later.

Sanderson's theory of a present underwater civilization and the speculation that UFOs are from that area may seem incredible. But such fantasies often have roots of truth, even if that truth comes from occult sources.

Spirit entities aren't bound by time. Satan can provide knowledge about the ancient past as well as the future.

We accept these theories only to the point where they can be supported by Scripture. There is biblical evidence that a world or civilization of a different order exists beneath the sea and that some of its visitors have a profound influence on our world.

Later in this book, we'll examine the biblical evidence. But for the moment, let's see what noted clairvoyants say.*

What Clairvoyants Say

EDGAR CAYCE—Edgar Cayce said there's a sunken metropolis under the sea near Bimini Island, fifty miles east of Miami. He believed that life originated on the lost continent of Atlantis and that we today have been reincarnated through many "entities" into our present forms. He calls these "our Atlantean Reincarnations."

Cayce was born on a farm near Hopkinsville, Kentucky, on March 18, 1877. He died on January 3, 1945, at the age of sixty-seven. From the age of twenty-five, over a period of forty-three years, he left more than fourteen thousand documented stenographic records of telepathic clairvoyant statements he had given to more than eight thousand people.

He refers to these typewritten documents as "readings." He made the readings after he went into a hypnotic sleep and was able to "see" his subjects in the light of their past, present and future "entities."

It was through these readings that Cayce predicted peoples' futures on the basis of their past lives in other forms and places.

At the age of six or seven Cayce told his parents he was able to "see" and talk to visions. At the age of twenty-one, in 1898, he became a salesman for a wholesale stationery company. About this time he developed a gradual paralysis of the throat muscles, which threatened the loss of his voice. When doctors were unable to find any physical cause, they tried hypnosis. But this also failed to help.

As the last resort Cayce asked a friend to help him

---

* By quoting these occultists the authors do not wish to imply any endorsement of their practices, as the reader will presently see.

reenter the same kind of hypnotic sleep that enabled him to memorize his schoolbooks as a child. Once he was into this trance, he solved his own problem by recommending medication and manipulative therapy, which successfully restored his voice and cured his throat trouble. Following this method he was able to cure the ailments of thousands of other people until his death in 1945.

From 1923, for the last twenty-two years of Cayce's life, Atlantis "readings" started to appear. They cover everything from technology, geography, names of people and the final destruction of Atlantis.

Cayce had three destructive periods for the lost continent, the last because "divine beings" invaded the bodies of pre-Adamic creatures and animals for their own "self-aggrandizement." He calls the "divine beings" who possessed the bodies of earthly creatures "Sons of Belial" and those who abstained "The Sons of Law I."

DARWIN GROSS—Called the living Eck Master, he says he saw the "light" when he was about to crash with his car years ago as another "pair of hands" grabbed the wheel; he came out of the incident alive and devoted to the one who helped him—Eckankar.

Eckankar is called the ancient science of soul travel.

"This organization is ancient because the movement had its origins on the *lost continent of Atlantis*," he says. Eckankar's headquarters is in Menlo Park, California, and has opened many new offices around the world.

ED SNEDEKER—One of the first solutions presented about the Triangle mystery came from the "third eye" of Ed Snedeker, a Connecticut psychic. Snedeker says he knows where everybody went in the Triangle twilight zone; he has been in "touch" with them. The psychic says he not only has seen them, but has talked with some of them. Although they

The Bible and

are invisible and will never be seen on Earth again, they are present; and their voices can be heard.

One of the men whom Snedeker is said to have contacted was an RAF pilot who got into the Triangle around 1945.

"When I searched for him and found him in 1969 he was still *alive*," Snedeker says. "Know where he was? Somewhere *down within the hollow of the Earth!*" [19]

M. B. DYKSHOORN—Dykshoorn of Miami, Florida, sees a giant whirlpool that originates from a *hole* in the *ocean floor* in the Triangle, which, when it reaches the surface, pulls in all of the surrounding air and airplanes as high as ten thousand feet, big ships and anything that floats, leaving no trace. [20]

Could this hole be the entrance to a subterranean world?

PAGE BRYANT—A seeress who has allegedly predicted many events accurately, says an unknown energy force dematerializes aircraft and huge ships in the Bermuda Triangle and permits UFOs to enter and exit the Earth.

Mrs. Bryant, through the transmedium of psychometry, concludes that the Triangle is a vortex of an unknown energy field that draws its power from other planets and the magnetic field of Earth.

Her conclusions have come after two flights over the Triangle and subsequent hypnosis to probe what she experienced. She says the Triangle is where UFOs enter and leave the Earth.

"This entire area is the vortex of a magnetic anomaly that allows those UFOs to enter and take off from Earth's atmosphere. On the first flight (into the Triangle), I saw below us—in my mind, while I was in the trance—an underwater base or cave. I felt it was being used as a UFO base."

She sees the Triangle as a tube of energy that extends

26

through the section of the Atlantic called the Bermuda Triangle, to its corresponding sector in the Pacific south of Japan known as the Devil's Sea where many ships also have disappeared under mysterious circumstances.

What happens to those who enter this energy zone?

"They dematerialize, pass on into another dimension," she says. "They're dead to us on this plane, but their energies, their spirits, go on. I know because on the first flight we made over the Triangle, I made transmedium contact with one of the gunners who disappeared December 5, 1945. His name is Robert Francis Gallivan, and during one of the hypnosis sessions, he told me:

" 'My God, let me tell what's happened!' " [21]

Misplaced Persons

The Bible has many similarities and correlations to these statements.

Cayce has three destructions of the Earth due to a "fall" of the divine into the carnal. The Bible lists two destructions due to "a lifting up of pride" and the intermarriage of angels with mankind. (See appendix.)

Cayce, Snedeker and Bryant say they have been in contact with departed spirits in the area of the Triangle. The Bible's Sheol-Hades is a place of departed spirits and is under the sea, as we shall see later.

Gross says his movement has its origins in Atlantis. The Bible speaks of disembodied spirits, which possibly had their release at the destruction and fall of Lucifer, God's archangel. These spirits are still in the world today and are capable of transferring supernatural acts to men.

Dykshoorn sees a hole in the Earth. One of the meanings of the Bible's Sheol-Hades is literally a subterranean pit or hole. Another meaning, which follows more closely to the root of the word "Sheol," is "a place of enquiry." If the entrance into the nether world is in the Triangle, it is significant to note how much mystery and curiosity has been aroused in the last few years in that area.

Plato says Poseidon (who held the name Neptune in the Roman pantheon) was the king of the ancient civilization Atlantis and that he sacrificed horses. Could this be the biblical Lucifer, the anointed cherub that covereth the whole Earth (Ezek. 28:14)?

Is there a connection between "horse latitudes" that run through the Sargasso Sea and the scorpion centaurs (half horse) which arise out of the bottomless pit during the tribulation period predicted in Revelation? Their king is Abaddon, meaning "destruction."

The Bible includes a nether world in these prophetical words:

> Therefore also God highly exalted him (Christ), and bestowed on Him the name which is above every name, that at the name of Jesus every knee should bow, of those who are in heaven, and on earth, and under the earth . . . (Phil. 2:9-10).

> And the sea gave up the dead which were in it . . . (Rev. 20:13).

Chapter 2

The Lost Cities

I looked on the earth, and behold, it was formless and void . . . a wilderness, and all its cities were pulled down . . . (Jer. 4:23-26).

To escape present realities, man lives in the nostalgia of the past. He loves to reminisce about the more secure periods of childhood, his home, school and his friends.

So it is with Lucifer, the angelic fugitive from God's kingdom known today as Satan or the devil.

Lucifer's beginning was blessed—the Bible calls him "perfect in beauty" and "an anointed cherub that covereth." He was perfect in all his ways until sin was found in him. He then became a fugitive, alien from the kingdom of God. He has never turned loose of his claims to his first estate; he relives it again and again through the lives of those who choose his religion of works over God's salvation through grace.

Biblical prophecies concerning the coming of God's kingdom are being fulfilled. The reality of that fact puts fear in the hearts of the fallen angelic beings and spirits who once lived on Earth under Lucifer's reign. They take seclusion in the dreams of their former home as their leader propagates "religions" that support this fantasy.

As part of his judgment, Lucifer's world was destroyed by flood.

Two Floods

There were two universal destructions in the ancient past, both by floods: the Luciferian Flood took place between 11,000 and 9,000 B.C. and climaxed the ice age, while the Noahic Flood was between 7000 and 5000 B.C. and brought to an end the Antediluvians of Noah's day. (See appendix.)

The Bible gives brief glimpses of the effect of the Luciferian Flood. Beginning with Gen. 1:2, Earth is covered with "waters" and is "without form and void." Dry land does not appear until the renovation of Earth in the ninth and tenth verses "and let the dry land appear: . . . And God called the dry land earth. . . ." (See appendix.)

The Bible also gives a brief look at the pre-Adamic social system. II Pet. 3:6 says, "Whereby the world that then was, being overflowed with water, perished." (See appendix.) The Greek word for world here is *kosmos*—a social system in contrast to another Greek word for world, *ge*, in verse seven, which means dirt. This social system was ruled by God's majestic angel of light—Lucifer.

Lucifer's kingdoms are recorded in Isa. 14:12-15 and Ezek. 28:11-19. Isaiah considers him the head of the pre-Adamic civilization, for he had a "throne" and had "weakened the nations." Ezekiel likens him to the King of Tyrus of his day when he says:

1. Lucifer was full of wisdom.

2. Perfect in beauty.
3. Had been in Eden.
4. Stones were his covering.
5. He was a virtuoso with a song ("workmanship of thy *tabrets* and of thy pipes").
6. He was an anointed cherub, speaking of a kingly angel set in a high office.
7. A covering cherub, which could signify stewardship over a possession—a protector.
8. He had sanctuaries.
9. He was in the Garden of Eden (his fall was *prior* to the temptation of Adam and Eve, for he was already in a fallen state in the form of a serpent).

Jesus saw this majestic angel of light fall "as lightning falling from heaven" (Luke 10:18). John the revelator says Lucifer took a third of the angels with him, which possibly were under his reign on the Earth (Rev. 12:4).

The *"without form"* and *"void"* of Gen. 1:2 is from two Hebrew words *tohu* and *bohu*. "Without form"—*tohu*—means disorganized and chaotic, while "void"—*bohu*—means empty and lifeless. (See appendix.)

Darkness was upon the deep (abyssmal oceans), because something cataclysmic had happened when that civilization, using Plato's words, had perished "in a day and a night" by a deluge.

Jeremiah uses these same words, "without form and void," (Jer. 4:23-26), in conjunction with:

1. Heavens which give no light.
2. Mountains and hills rearranged through earthquakes and volcanic upheavals.
3. Formerly fruitful places which have become a wilderness.
4. Cities broken down.
5. The disappearance of birds and men.

The second universal flood was the Noahic deluge in Genesis 7.

This time it was for the wickedness of man and of fallen angels who had intermarried with the human race (Gen. 6:1-4). These spirits are now kept in hell (Gr. *Tartarus*) in the nether world (II Pet. 2:4-5). The Earth was reshaped during both of these upheavals; continents and land masses were shifted. (See appendix.)

Let us now examine the evidences of these upheavals.

The Rocks Cry Out

The Earth's crust records tremendous cataclysmic upheavals in its recent history. The Earth's radius is 3,959 miles; 2,160 miles of which is the core. The mantle is 870 miles thick, and the Mohorovicic discontinuity or "skin" is about 30 miles thick.

Scientist J. Tuzo Wilson suggests that the "moho" was the original surface of Earth, while Whitcomb and Morris say the core and mantle could be the biblical foundations spoken of in Job 38:4-7. God said to Job, "Were you there when the foundations of the Earth were laid?" The implication is that God was the only eyewitness.

The crust varies from sixteen to forty-four miles; it is thickest beneath the land continents, and thinnest under the *oceans*, especially the Indian and Atlantic oceans where it is sixteen and twenty-two miles in places.

The Earth's crust was formed by volcanic action, mountain folds and uplift, and sedimentation (geosynclines, alluvial plains, deposition and lithification). Sedimentation and erosion are the chief deluge agents along with vast volcanic and mountain upheavals.[1]

MAJOR VOLCANIC ERUPTIONS—There are perhaps five hundred active volcanoes in the world today and possibly three times that many are extinct, but nothing ever seen by man today can be compared with the formation of such

EARTH'S COMPOSITION

This chart shows the different elements that compose our planet. The Earth's crust is thinnest beneath the seas. Author's chart.

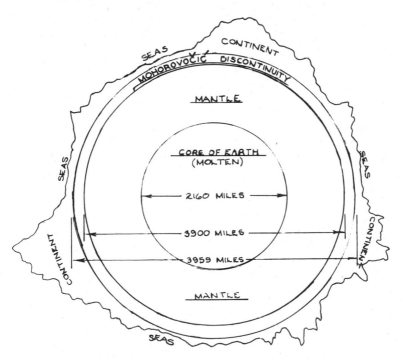

CRUST

Varies from 16-44 miles thick. It is thickest under continents—thinnest under oceans, especially the Indian and Atlantic, 16-22 miles.

Gates to Sheol-Hades at the earth's thinnest crust areas under the seas!

MOHOROVIČIĆ DISCONTINUITY

Named after its founder who first founded its existence in 1909. It has an average thickness of 30 miles.

This was the original earth. The crust was caused by volcanic, seismic and mountain upheavals according to Henry M. Morris in *The Genesis Flood* (p. 219).

structures as the Columbian Plateau and the Canadian Shield.

THE COLUMBIA PLATEAU—In Washington and Oregon remains of an enormous volcanic eruption cover two hundred thousand square miles with a lava flow two thousand feet thick in some places. This happened in recent geological history because some of the old peaks rise out of this lava bed.

CANADIAN SHIELD—There are many great volcanic shields in the world, and one of the biggest in the North American continent is the Canadian Shield. It comprises two million square miles of lava flow. Only a tremendous catastrophe could cause this kind of eruption; nothing in the present day compares with this.[2]

CRUSTAL MOVEMENTS—Great thicknesses of rocks are uplifted thousands of feet, strata are buckled, folded, sometimes have been thrust laterally or completely overturned on a gigantic scale. Such is the case in the Rocky Mountain Chain and the Appalachian System.

APPALACHIAN SYSTEM—Believed to be the uplifted and eroded remnant of a great geosynclinal trough in which a thickness of some forty thousand feet of sedimentary rocks was deposited. The crust of the Earth seems to have been distorted, fractured, elevated, depressed and contorted in almost every conceivable way at some time or times in the past.

SEAMOUNTS—Many of these have been found in the last few years. These are nothing more than drowned islands in the middle of the ocean.

SUBMARINE CANYONS—These are canyons that were cut *before* the ocean basins were depressed during the deluge period. Two deep undersea canyons were formed by the Hudson River off of New York, with a depth of fifteen thousand feet, and the Congo River off West Africa. The biblical record of deluge conditions is the only answer for their origin. As Whitcomb and Morris say:

> As the lands were uplifted and the ocean basins depressed at the close of the Deluge period, the great currents streaming down into the ocean depths would quickly have eroded great gorges in the still soft and unconsolidated sediments exposed by the sinking basins. Then as these gorges were themselves submerged by the continuing influx of waters from the rising continental blocks, it may well have been that the turbidity currents entering the canyons may have deepened and extended them still further—a process that has continued on a smaller scale since then.[3]

GLACIERS—The two present-day glaciers are in Greenland and the Antarctica, but nothing compares with the great ice sheets of the past—some four million square miles of North America and two million miles of Europe were glaciated.

ALLUVIAL SLOPE—This is formed or produced by the action of rivers. The central region of the United States, known as the Great Plains, consists of one great alluvial plain. This mass of deposits was laid down by heavy-laden rivers coming down from the recently uplifted Rocky Mountains to the west. The surface produced by this alluviation is as flat as any land surface in nature. Many thousands of square miles in the Llano Estacado or Staked Plains of Texas and New Mexico, an area of twenty thousand square miles, are almost untouched by erosion. There are widespread deposits, either alluvial or deltaic in nature, of a magnitude far beyond that of any deposits now being formed. Only waters of a universal flood magnitude can account for ancient deposits as they are found.

UPLIFTS—These have puzzled students of Earth's crust for a long time. The Colorado Plateau uplift is described by Fenneman:

> The first distinguishing feature is approximate horizontality of its rocks. . . . The second distinguishing feature of the province is great elevation. Aside from canyon bottoms, no considerable portion of it is lower than 5,000 feet. . . . Between this and 11,000 feet, there are plateaus of all altitudes, some of them being higher than the nearby mountain ranges.[4]

This region occupies about 250,000 square miles, including most of Utah and Arizona, with large segments of Colorado and New Mexico. As Whitcomb and Morris point out, the remarkable thing is that this region has somehow been uplifted from far below sea level (these sediments on the whole are of marine origin) to more than a mile above sea level, without disturbing the horizontality of the strata or summit levels. And this happened not once, but many times.

The Tibetan Plateaus create a similar problem only on a much larger scale. Here we have a former marine area of 750,000 square miles raised roughly three miles above sea level. The Himalayan mountain chain bordering this region has floated upward some five miles.

Whitcomb and Morris conclude:

> It seems much more likely that the sediments all were deposited more or less rapidly and continuously, followed by a single great regional uplift. Subsequent rapid canyon downcutting then ensued

When Surtesy erupted in 1963, a cloud of ash and gases arose from the ocean. Submarine eruptions are often so violent that the cone of the volcano appears above the surface, forming an islet. Scores more remain beneath the surface and are known as sea-mounts. Their number indicates that, at one time, volcanic activity was very intense. Photo: Sigurdur Thorarinsson.

while the sediments were still relatively soft and the rivers were carrying much larger discharges.[5]

Mouth to Fossil Resuscitation

Oil and coal are formed by decayed living organisms, either plant or animal, sometimes under extreme pressure or heat. Yet when one looks into modern-day geological columns, there are no modern-day parallels now going on in the Earth's crust that compare with the forces which created these immense coal and oil fields.

Only a cataclysmic plow could turn this much material into the rocks of the Earth to await heat, pressure and decay.

A uniform time scale over billions of years cannot answer the problems of "displaced" fossils, the appearance of primitive creatures in our day and the origin of great mountain chains; only a universal flood can answer these questions.

Fossil graveyards around the world speak out for a universal flood. Certain conditions have to be present for fossils to be formed and preserved.

First, preservation of the entire organism by freezing. For the flesh of an animal to keep for thousands of years it *must* be frozen in less than thirty minutes. Our frozen foods must be quick-frozen or they would spoil. Estimates have shown that the remains of up to five million mammoths are buried along the coasts of Siberia and Alaska. Russian scientists reportedly have actually eaten the meat of these behemoths! The mammoths had to be buried suddenly and catastrophically to be preserved for so long.

Second, preservation of only the *hard parts* of the organism. Never does one find, in our present generation, great graveyards of organisms buried together and waiting for fossilization. But this is exactly the sort of thing that has occurred in these fossil deposits around the world. Take for instance the following:

LINCOLN COUNTY, WYOMING—Here fish and palm leaves, from six to eight feet long and from three to four feet wide have been uncovered. This speaks of a tropical climate completely opposite to the blizzard-ridden mountains that are there now. In 1890 an alligator was found there, plus several garpike, ranging in size from four to six feet; birds, sunfish, rasp-tongues, deep sea bass, chubs, pickerel, herring, mollusca, turtles, mammals and many varieties of insects.

Fish, no less than other creatures, do not naturally become entombed like this but are usually quickly devoured by other fish after dying. I. Velikovsky, in his book *Earth in Upheaval*, says:

When a fish dies its body floats on the surface or sinks to the bottom and is devoured rather quickly, actually in a matter of hours, by other fish; however, the fossil fish found in sedimentary rocks is very often preserved with all its bones intact. Entire shoals of fish over large areas numbering billions of specimens are found in a state of agony, but with no mark of a scavenger's attack. [6]

M. Brogersma-Sanders says: "The life of most animals in the sea is terminated by their capture by other animals; those that die in other ways are sooner or later eaten by scavengers."[7]

FLORISSANT, COLORADO—Here we evidently have volcanic dust that showered down upon myriads of a wide variety of insects, which are preserved in rocks of volcanic shale.

CUMBERLAND BONE CAVE—This cavern in Maryland contains a mixture of fossils from different temperature zones. From those which are found in the Arctic regions we have the wolverine, grizzly bear and mustelidae; from the prairie regions, fossils such as peccaries, tapirs, antelope, ground hogs, rabbits and coyotes. From the more humid regions, there are the beaver and muskrat.

Other caves in the same region, within three miles, are barren of fossils. This suggests a catastropic event which brought together organisms from entirely different habitats and different climatic regions in one great mass. This is characteristic of many of the fossil graveyards.

BALTIC AMBER DEPOSITS—Multitudes of insects, flowers and other organisms are present which belong to all regions of the Earth's surface.

LIGNITE BEDS OF GEISELTAL, GERMANY—Again a complete mixture of plants, insects and animals from all climatic zones and all regions of the world.

OTHER AREAS—The Karroo formation of South Africa with 800 million skeletons of vertebrate animals; the La Brea Tar Pits in Los Angeles, California; the Sicilian hippopotamus beds with fossils so extensive they have been mined for commercial use; the Rocky Mountain mammal beds and the Dinosaur beds in North Dakota and the Gobi Desert.[8]

We could go on, but space will not permit us to show how only hydraulic processes could form oil and coal, how petrification with casts and molds of materials could have only been formed by flooding action.

How did the Petrified Forest form in the middle of the Arizona desert in southwestern United States?

How did vast amounts of oil form under Pudhoe Bay in Alaska, which is now a barren, bleak icy waste near the Arctic? Were these beds water-shafted from other parts of the world, or was this area once a steaming jungle that was turned under?

Again, fossils that have been buried around the world

could have only been deposited by a deluge. The sedimentation of rivers collects in the eddies and bays and is there deposited much the same way that a universal flood would have deposited specimens together from all over the world.

The Past Is a Key to the Present

True geology agrees with the biblical record of a universal flood. Many geologists, however, have refused to accept a sudden, all-engulfing flood. Local upheavals on a minor scale, yes, but not a world-wide deluge.

They have been the disciples of the "High Priest of Uniformitarianism" Charles Lyell (1797-1875); he blew his first blast of the uniformitarian trumpet in 1830 when he said geologic processes now operating in Earth had been active for extremely long periods in the past, and such gradual processes could account for the world as we see it today, without the need of appealing to sudden and stupendous catastrophies.

Lyell was an advocate of William "Strata" Smith (1769-1839), "The Father of Stratigraphic Geology," and James Hutton (1726-1797) whose "divine" phrase, "The present is the key to the past," guides the scientific world today. Lyell says:

> All theories are rejected which involve the assumption of sudden and violent catastrophies and revolutions of the whole earth, and its inhabitants. . . . [9]

Charles Darwin was a disciple of Lyell of whom he says, "He who can read Sir Charles Lyell's grand work on the Principles of Geology, which the future historian will recognize as having produced a revolution in natural science, and yet does not admit how vast have been the past periods of time, may at once close this volume."[10]

Francis C. Haber concludes, "There can be little doubt

that it was through Lyell's "Principles of Geology," that Darwin's mind was emancipated from the shackles of biblical chronology, and had this step not been taken, it seems unlikely that *The Origin of the Species* could ever have fermented out of the voyage of the *Beagle,* for Darwin's theory of evolution required for its foundation far more historical time than even the uniformitarian geologists were accustomed to conceiving."[11]

Six Million Dollar Man

Why do geologists and evolutionists want to deny a sudden universal biblical flood when the rocks and fossils cry out? Listen to a biblical prophecy written by Peter two thousand years ahead of his time!

Know this first of all, that in the last days mockers will come with *their* mocking, following after their own lusts, and saying, 'Where is the promise of His coming? . . . all continues just as it was from the beginning of creation' (divine uniformity). For when they maintain this, it escapes their notice that by the word of God *the* heavens existed long ago and *the* earth was formed out of water and by water, through which the world at that time was destroyed, being flooded with water . . . (II Pet. 3:3-6).

Scoffers have created the "six million dollar man," programmed and computed by man himself! From the single cell organism to the multi-cell genius!

For one to admit to any world-wide cataclysmic upheaval is to admit to a divine judgment. Once one does that he becomes responsible to a divine being and His moral laws. The pride of man rules out divine intervention at any time in

Earth's history for man wants to be responsible only to himself.

The Crystal Ball

The metaphysical societies all believe in a universal flood. Cayce had three destructive periods; Rosicrucianists believe whole continents slipped under the surface of the sea. Most of them trace their *origins*, either by reincarnation or some type of cosmic mind, back to these former civilizations.

Atlantis of the Atlantic and Lemuria of the Pacific are their chief hereditary birthplaces. They say these civilizations came from outer space—some by UFOs and others by gods of the Greek mythological type. Their forms and shapes vary from the present man, but the great promise is "that many of them are still in the world today." The rest of them are living in an underworld abode.

Cayce's accounts say the reason for the destruction was lust, "self-aggrandizement and intermarriage of divine/physical forms." The "good" didn't fall (Sons of Law I), but the "evil" did (Sons of Belial), and brought the antediluvian destruction upon themselves. Both of these "entities" are in the world today, and some are in an abode under the sea where their former home submerged.[12]

Sanderson, an advocate of the lost continent Atlantis, said there are civilizations under the oceans of the world. Life not only began in the water, but has in some cases remained there. And from time to time, these beings of superior intelligence pluck down to their abodes, for examination, samples of Earth's men and ships of today.[13] Is there a connection to these statements and the mysteries surrounding the Bermuda Triangle?

Cayce in one of his "readings" on June 28, 1940, predicted that portions of the lost continent Atlantis would rise again in 1968 or 1969. Cayce's followers are quick to point out that Dr. Manson Valentine, former professor of zoology at Yale, reported in 1968-1970 that he had made discoveries in the Bermuda Triangle of Mayan-like temples in the Bahamian waters off the coast of Florida, a plaza and sloping walls with steps.

Dr. Valentine believes that the pyramid-like structures might be part of a sunken continent. A one hundred-foot pentagon, also, was found near the site of a temple-like building near Andros Island as well as a road, stone wheels and a statuary.[14]

Berlitz says that numerous road causeways have often been seen from the air off the coast of Yucatan, Mexico, site of an ancient civilization. They leave the shore in straight lines going toward unknown underwater locations farther out to sea in deeper waters. Also, the deep sea diving submarine *Aluminaut*, on a 1967 mission off Florida, Georgia and South Carolina, observed an enormous underwater road or pavement that has previously been above water. Berlitz goes on to say:

> The road was apparently formed of, or paved with, manganese oxide and, when special wheels were installed on the Aluminaut it was able to proceed along the road, which in some places reached a depth of three thousand feet, as if the Aluminaut were a car driving along a normal road, except that the road was, in this case, at the bottom of the sea. The size of the paved surface was too large to suggest the conclusion that it had been man-made as was also the case with a very extensive "tiled" section of the ocean bottom observed by Dr. Bruce Heezen of the Lamont Observatory, while making a deep dive in the Bahama area.[15]

Prehistoric aircraft? This 1,800-year-old artifact from a tomb in South America is considered by some people to be a model of an ancient airplane. A copy is on display in the permanent World of Man Exhibit in Montreal. Photo: Jack Ullrich.

An article in the March 24, 1975 issue of *The Daily Breeze* (a Torrance, California, suburban newspaper) confirms that a civilization existed off the Bahamas more than six thousand years ago:

MIAMI (UPI)—A group of underwater explorers says a submerged rock formation off Bimini in the Bahamas is "the key that validates the myth of Atlantis."

The International Explorers Society says it is prepared to prove the "Bimini Road" dates back more than six thousand years.

"As far as we are concerned, Atlantis is a myth, but our job in the International Explorers Society is to explore the various relationships," said Jim Woodman, the group's director.

The book of *Dzyan*, supposed to have originated beyond the Himalayas (its teachings have reached the eastern world of Japan, India, and China), states:

Large areas of land sank in the ocean off present-day Cuba and Florida in 9564 B.C. [16]

Others sites of possible ancient civilizations include the Mound Builders of America, the plateau of El Enladrillade in Chile, Island of Santa Rosa in California, the mountains of Ennedi in Southern Sahara and the remains of Yucatan, Mexico.

Another lost continent that gets a lot of publicity from the occult is called Lemuria; it purportedly slipped beneath the waters of the Pacific Ocean.

W.S. Cerve in *Lemuria, the Lost Continent of the Pacific*, claimed a civilization lived on this continent until its destruction. Lemurians lived in an advanced culture with large buildings, temples, transportation by boats; they supposedly had large heads with a third eye in the middle of the forehead like a tumorous growth. Lumerians used the appendage for "cosmic ability" to communicate psychically—a form of mental telepathy. This civilization, Cerve says, was the beginning of "beings" which still exist today; in fact many of the people of California come from this prehistoric culture! [17]

While geological evidence does support the idea of a

continent under the Atlantic, there is little comparable data for a former continent beneath the Pacific.

In Plato's dialogue there was a maritime king named Poseidon. Poseidon's home was Atlantis with all of its Edenic beauty. Plato did not invent the name of Poseidon; the worship of Poseidon was universal in the earliest ages of Europe. Ernest Curtius, quoted by John Denison Baldwin, says: "Poseidon worship seems to have been a peculiarity of all the colonies previous to the time of Sidon."[18]

Curtius says this worship was carried to Spain and to Northern Africa, but most abundantly to Italy, to many of the islands and regions around the Aegean Sea.

Poseidon is represented in Greek mythology as a *sea god;* a standing figure drawn by horses in a chariot. Donnelly says:

> Poseidon was a sea god because he ruled over a great land in the sea, and was the national god of a maritime people. He is associated with horses because in Atlantis the horse was first domesticated with race courses and chariots which were invented by them. . . .[19]

Donnelly, referring to Plato's dialogues, says horses were the favorite sacrifice of Poseidon; they were killed and cast into the sea from high precipices. The religious horse-feasts of the pagan Scandinavians were a survival of this Poseidon worship, which once prevailed along the coasts of Europe until suppressed by Christianity.

Not only was Poseidon represented as a sea god drawn by war horses, but upon his head was a trident crown. The three-pronged scepter of Poseidon reappears constantly in ancient history. We find it in the hands of the Hindu gods and at the base of the religious beliefs of antiquity. According to Arthur Schott:

Among the numerals, sacred three has ever been considered the mark of perfection and was therefore exclusively ascribed to the Supreme Deity, or to its earthly representative—a king, emperor or a sovereign. For this reason triple emblems of various shapes are found in belts, neckties or any encircling fixture, as can be seen on the works of ancient art in Yucatan, Guatemala, Chiapas, Mexico, etc. Wherever the object has reference to divine supremacy, we are reminded of the Tiara and the triple round of sovereignty.[21]

The Father, Son and Holy Spirit comprise the Trinity of the Bible ("These three bear record in heaven" I John 5:7). Poseidon's triple crown could represent the supremacy of the Godhead. It was Lucifer's claim to this position that brought the deluge to his kingdom (Isa. 14:13-15).

Could Poseidon and the biblical Lucifer be the same person? Could the lost continent Atlantis, where Poseidon ruled, and the nations and cities of Lucifer's reign be the same?

If so, it would explain the importance which the occult, television, and the movies ("The Poseidon Adventure" and "The Chariots of the Gods") are placing on the Bermuda Triangle.

Just before the climactic battle of Armageddon (Rev. 16:16), Earth is controlled by a "beast" out of the sea whom Bible commentators call "Antichrist" (Rev. 13:1). This is a different beast than the one which comes out of the Earth (Rev. 13:11), which is called the "false prophet" or which some say represents the false religious head of the coming one-world government.

The trident symbol reappears in the closing chapters of

Revelation in the form of a dragon, the beast and the false prophet (Rev. 16:13). This unholy trinity is the subject of the great final battle of Armageddon in which 200 million horses are involved.

It is Lucifer's last gasp, his last claim to a former civilization that he had ruled over.

As we go into the next few chapters, we are going to discover what is under the sea and note the Bible's correlations on Atlantis, Poseidon, horses and natural phenomena to the mystery of the Triangle.

Chapter 3

The Sargasso Sea

*Then Jonah prayed to the
LORD his God from the
stomach of the fish . . . I
cried for help from the
depth of Sheol . . . the
great deep engulfed me,
weeds were wrapped
around my head . . . the
earth with its bars was
around me . . . Thou
has brought up my life
from the pit, O Lord my
God (Jonah 2:1-6).*

Four signs point to the geographical location of a former continent in the Bermuda Triangle—the Sargasso Sea, migrating eels, submarine canyons and horses.

Could God's finger be pointing to a precise spot of immense importance? What is under the sea?

Discerning the Signs

There are physical and natural disturbances in the Scriptures that correlate spiritual truth. Biblical symbolism brings to light the truth it is trying to represent. The God who set the laws of the universe also made the moral laws of the Bible. And unless tampered with by man, they always will agree—never contradict.

Examples of this are found in the story of Job.

In the first chapter we are introduced to a righteous man named Job, who had seven sons, three daughters, 7,000 sheep, 3,000 camels, 500 yoke of oxen, 500 female donkeys and many servants.

The Bible says that there was a day when the sons of God came before the Lord and Satan came with them. In the discussion that followed between the Lord and Satan, the Lord said, "Have you considered My servant Job? For there is no one like him on the earth, a blameless and upright man. . . ." Satan then accused the Lord of putting a hedge about Job and all that he owned. "But put forth Thy hand now and touch all that he has; he will surely curse Thee to Thy face," Satan said.

The Lord answered, "Behold, all that he has is in your power, only do not put forth your hand on him" (Job 1:12).

NOW WATCH HOW A SUPERNATURAL BEING WORKS. He never comes out on front stage and says, "Here I am, folks; watch me do my act." He always works in accordance with natural laws or through individuals:

First, Sabeans attacked and took Job's animals (vs. 15).

Second, fire burned up the sheep and the servants (vs. 16).

Third, Chaldeans raided the camels and killed the servants (vs. 17).

Fourth, a great wind blew the house down (vs. 19).

Fifth, boils covered Job's body (vs. 2:7).

While some may attribute these incidents to mere natural phenomena, it is plain that all of these "physical" and "natural" disturbances were done by a supernatural being—Satan.

During World War II, when the British were surrounded in a little French fishing village called Dunkirk, a strange thing happened. These were the crack British regiments, the cream of the English army, which had fled before the onrushing German Panzers. If the Germans could capture these thousands of troops, they could possibly deliver the fatal blow to the British.

The Luftwaffe had command of the air, barring escape by sea. The troops seemed doomed. That day Sir Winston Churchill called his nation to prayer for the survival of their gallant men.

All of England's available small craft, from dinghies to fishing vessels, sailed across the channel in operation *Dynamo.*

Then it happened; a "natural" phenomenon of "smoke and clouds," [1] flowed in over the water sealing off the skies from the German Air Force. Under this umbrella, the rescue proceeded without interruption. World War II could have ended differently were it not for the "natural smoke and clouds" that rolled in that day.

An accident? Ask the English High Command. There were no atheists that day.[2]

Howard Flesher, owner of a back-hoe excavation company in Redondo Beach, California, recalls an incident that happened several years before the age of jet aircraft.

He was working near Los Angeles International Airport on an excavation in an alley behind a church. Unknown to him, a large, highly volatile high-pressure aviation gas line was under the ground in this area. As he put his backhoe into the excavation to take out more soil, he ruptured the pipe; immediately the area was engulfed in gas, which shot fifty feet into the air. Because of the tremendous pressure, it turned into a highly volatile fog. One spark and the whole city block would explode. He quickly sent his man for help while he back-filled the excavation.

"The ominous fog started to roll into the church, under the doors and through the windows. I knew if it reached any appliances with gas pilots, the church would explode," Flesher says.

Then a strange thing happened.

"It was like an unseen hand; the fog mysteriously started to roll back out of the church and the windows in an opposite direction."

"It beats anything I've ever seen," he says.

The changing of the air flow, a *wind:* was this a freak accident of nature? Ask Howard Flesher; he knows it was an unseen hand!

Let us now examine the signs which point to the geographical location of a former continent in the Triangle.

Sargasso Sea

Could the Sargasso Sea be a *sign* of something that happened in the past?

Sailors recount the unnerving legends of the "sea of fear," "sea of lost ships" and "graveyard of lost ships." The legends say this graveyard contained ships from all nations, which were caught and immobilized in the fields of seaweed, with borer worms eating the holds, still manned by skeleton crews.

Death, they say, came to tramp steamers, yachts, whalers, clippers, packets, brigantines, pirate vessels and—to make their stories more appealing—to the adventuresome Spanish treasure galleons.

While our text in Jonah is descriptive of the sea and the fish, it has similarity with the Sargasso Sea.

The word "sargasso" comes from the Portuguese word for several species of gulfweed. The sargassum (generic term for gulfweed), which floats either separately or in large masses, marks the boundary of this sea with the Western Atlantic.

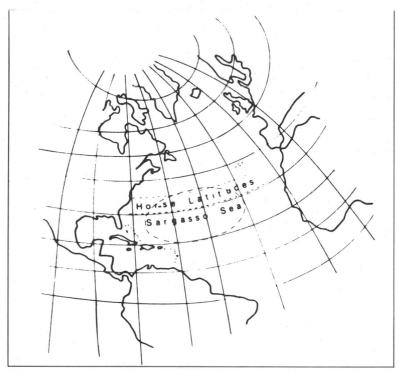

The Horse Latitudes were so named by ancient mariners who had to jettison their war horses for lack of drinking water when their ships were becalmed in these latitudes, which, as the map shows, correspond roughly to the boundaries of the Sargasso Sea. The map is taken from *The Bermuda Triangle Mystery—Solved* by David Kusche, copyright © 1975 by Lawrence David Kusche, and used by permission of Harper & Row, Publishers.

This area has been called a funnel, a vortex, a whirlpool and a hole with a lid marked by these floating seaweeds—as if this was a place of refuse marked by a stagnant calm of sargassum.

A description of the Sargasso Sea is given by Berlitz in *The Bermuda Triangle.*

"This seaweed sea is bounded on the north by the Gulf

Stream as it moves first northeast and then east and on the west and south by the returning Gulf Stream and the North Equatorial Current," he says.

"Although somewhat amorphous, it extends from about 37° north latitude to about 27° south latitude and from 75° west to 40° east. Under the deep waters of the Sargasso Sea lie the Hatteras and Nares Abyssal plains, the precipitous Bermuda Rise, numerous mysterious seamounts (underwater mountains rising toward the surface but terminating in flat tops as if they had once been islands), and at its eastern limits, part of the North Atlantic Ridge, a tremendous north-south underwater mountain chain in the middle of the Atlantic Ocean whose highest crests break through the surface of the sea to form the Azores Islands. In other words, a stagnant sea almost devoid of currents except on its borders, extends from about two hundred miles north of the Greater Antilles up the Florida and Atlantic coasts at a general distance of about two hundred miles from land to the vicinity of Cape Hatteras and then out in the Atlantic in the direction of the Iberian Peninsula and Africa up to the North Atlantic Ridge and back again to the Americas." [3]

The Sargasso Sea seaweed is carried north-northeast from off the coast of Florida in the Gulf Stream, then south by the returning Gulf Stream and the north equatorial currents. This forms a giant vortex of floating seaweed whose mass covers an area of 1.5 million square miles. Occultists believe this is the residue of vegetation that floated on the surface of the ocean when the lost continent Atlantis sank.

The Sinuous Trail of Eels

Each year North American and European eels migrate to the depths of the Bermuda Triangle. Some suggest the eels at one time were like salmon, which go out to sea and return again to spawn. They came up the rivers and tributaries of the lost continent Atlantis until it finally submerged beneath the sea. Now they still return to spawn in the same place, but in the depths of the sea where Atlantis once existed.

Here is an interesting Scripture in this context:

> Though they dig into Sheol, From there shall My hand take them; And though they ascend to heaven, From there will I bring them down. And though they hide on the summit of Carmel, I will search them out and take them from there; and though they conceal themselves from My sight on the floor of the sea, from there I will command the serpent and it will bite them . . . (Amos 9:2-3).

Here is a Scripture that connects the underworld compartment, Sheol, and the serpent in the bottom of the sea. It was a serpent in the Garden of Eden that ensnared Eve. This same creature is used in Rev. 20:2 as a description of Satan.

It is interesting to note the connection between the stagnant refuse pool and sinuous serpentine eels that migrate there and the Scripture which links sea serpents with Sheol, an underground abode of departed spirits.

Submarine Rivers

Huge canyons continue out under the ocean at the mouths of the Hudson, Delaware, St. Lawrence and Congo Rivers. It would seem that it took more than underwater turbid currents to form these vast undersea gorges. It is suggested that these were formed above water and that when the continents shifted, they also submerged under the sea.

Could it be that these are another sign pointing to the Bermuda Triangle?

Horses

The last of these signs is horses. According to Cayce and Donnelly, the horse was first domesticated and used for racing on Atlantis. Poseidon's chariot was drawn by two horses.

Horses also were sacrificed in ancient religious ceremonies. (Sheep, oxen and goats were used in the Jewish sacrificial system, never horses. The Hebrews were at first forbidden to keep horses they captured [4] and accordingly hamstrung most of those that Joshua took in the battle for Canaan.) [5]

Geographically, the northern Horse Latitude runs directly through the Sargasso Sea over the migratory spot of the eels. These latitudes run in the northern and southern hemispheres, 30° latitude from the equator. Sailors aboard becalmed ships had to destroy and dump their war horses overboard to conserve water. Berlitz says:

> Modern motor ships no longer run the risk of being becalmed—a fact that makes the numerous ship disappearances there even more mysterious. Of course *all* ship losses are mysterious inasmuch as relatively few captains set out to lose their ships. When the fate of a ship is established or even assumed, the mystery ceases. This has not been the case with the many ships that have disappeared in the Sargasso Sea. [6]

In the Bible, God used curses that parallel man's disobedience in idolatry. God creates a curse in the form of the very mode of that false worship. Take, for instance, the ten plagues upon the Egyptians brought through Moses. Each of the plagues was upon one of the ten Egyptian deities.

The plague of turning the Nile River into blood (Exodus 7:19-25), was very humiliating, inasmuch as they were so dependent upon the Nile for water that it was worshipped through the fertility god, Osiris.

The plague of frogs (Exodus 8:1-4), was very aggravating to the Egyptians, for the frog was included among the sacred animals. It was sacred to the goddess Hekt, who bore the head of the frog.

The staff that Moses cast upon the ground became a crocodile (not a serpent), according to many commentators (Heb. *tannin*—dragon). The crocodile was one of the Egyptians' chief deities, and this plague showed that God is the creator of the creatures of the Nile.

God will use horses in His last judgment upon the Earth. The most severe of the judgments upon the nations comes from the fifth and sixth trumpet judgments predicted in the Book of Revelation.

In the fifth trumpet God looses demon scorpion horses to sting men for six months; these horses come up out of the bottomless pit under the sea (Rev. 9:1-11).

Could God be bringing judgment upon Poseidon's former kingdom out of the midst of the sea where he once reigned?

In the sixth trumpet judgment about two hundred million horses fight in the final battles of Earth "with blood up to their bridles." The chapter closes with these words:

> And the rest of mankind, who were not killed by these plagues, did not repent of the works of their hands, so as not to worship demons, and the idols of gold and of silver and of brass and of stone and of wood, which can neither see nor hear nor walk; and they did not repent of their murders nor of their sorceries nor of their immorality nor of their thefts.
> . . . (Rev. 9:20-21).

The four horsemen of the Apocalypse ride on white, red, black and ashen horses in the first seal judgments (Rev. 6:1-8). The same colored horses are seen in Zech. 1:11; 6:2-7 in conjunction with angelic patrols on the Earth.

The Lord counters with his white horses coming in the clouds to fight with Antichrist at Armageddon (Rev. 19:11-21).

If Poseidon (Lucifer) once ruled the Earth from the continent Atlantis, and it was on this continent that horses were sacrificed, could it be that the horse judgments are God's curse upon the sea and its surroundings?

Again, we ask the questions in the light of these signs: Is God's finger pointing to a place in the sea of immense significance?

What is under the sea?

Chapter 4

The Devil's Triangle

Those who go down to the sea in ships, Who do business on great waters; They have seen the works of the LORD, and His wonders in the deep.

For He spoke and raised up a stormy wind, Which lifted up the waves of the sea . . . They reeled and staggered like a drunken man, And were at their wits' end. . . . He caused the storm to be still, So that the waves of the sea were hushed.

Then they were glad because they were quiet; So He guided them to their desired haven (Psa. 107:23-30).

For thousands of years, mysteries have surrounded the area of the Bermuda Triangle.[1]

But are these mysteries so mysterious? Or are they the speculations and lies of cultists and sensationalists? And if they are lies, who's lying and why?

61

The Triangle is a 200,000-square-mile area off the Atlantic coast. Its apexes are the Virgin Islands near Puerto Rico, Bermuda and a point in the Gulf of Mexico west of Florida.[2] In this area more than a hundred ships and planes are said to have disappeared, most of them since 1945.

The Federal Aviation Administration (FAA) says the idea that planes missing in the Triangle have been the victims of sinister forces is "nonsense." [3]

While it admits there are special problems associated with flying the Triangle, the FAA scoffs at the idea offered by a number of magazine articles and best-selling books that "flying into this mythical area is tantamount to sauntering through the gates of hell." [4]

While leading authorities agree on this point, we will reserve our conclusion for later.

There are many theories about the Triangle's alleged mysteries. One introduces questions, which only the Bible can answer.

Ron Libert of UFO Distributing Company, who was handling the distribution of the film "The Devil's Triangle," produced by Richard Winer, offered a $10,000 award to any viewer who could solve the mystery after the film completes its theatrical run. Winer cites a theory by James C. Jackson, Jr., of Portsmouth, Virginia, sent in response to the offer in his latest book on the Triangle:

> It's a passageway to another part of the Earth. Strange disappearances occur because supernatural beings want no one to know the secrets of Satan.[5]

In this chapter we will explore some of the Triangle theories and seek answers to the questions: "Is there really a mystery in the Triangle? If so, what is its secret?

Ghost Ship—In 1872 this sailing vessel, the *Mary Celeste*, was found abandoned in the Atlantic. The Bettmann Archive.

We believe the Bible has the answers—answers that, while not so mysterious, have eerie significance.

The FAA believes accidents and disappearances in the Triangle can be attributed to weather, inexperienced pilots and poor navigation equipment.

A publication prepared by the U.S. Coast Guard in Miami says, "It has been our experience that the combined forces of nature and the unpredictability of mankind outdo the most far-fetched science fiction."

The FAA contends that usually benign weather can change radically, with cyclical storms that can rip the wings off a plane and drop the pieces into the ocean. The Gulf

Stream can carry floating wreckage, ships or planes, miles away from the scene of an accident, frustrating search and rescue operations and giving rise to the speculations that have made the Triangle so mysterious.

The element of mystery begins to look incredible when we consider that much of it was deliberately manufactured or perpetuated by writers seeking to satisfy the human craving for the sensational.

"Many of the writers who publicized the events," says Lawrence David Kusche, "did no original research but merely rephrased the articles of previous writers, thereby perpetuating the errors and embellishments in earlier accounts. In a number of incidents writers withheld information that provided an obvious solution to the disappearance.

"The legend of the Bermuda Triangle is a manufactured mystery. It began because of careless research and was elaborated upon and perpetuated by writers who either purposely or unknowingly made use of misconceptions, faulty reasoning and sensationalism.

"I, like everyone else, like a good mystery, an enigma that stretches the mind. We all seem to have an innate desire to remain in awe of those phenomena for which there appears to be no logical scientific explanation. Yet we also exult in seeking and in finding legitimate answers to these same puzzles." [6]

Kusche also says the weather was bad when many of the incidents occurred, contrary to the legend. Hurricanes were responsible in some of the highly publicized cases. Years after some of the incidents occurred, writers found references to them and turned them into mystery; the truth is, however, when they occurred, the incidents were not considered mysterious.

Some disappearances remain a mystery, Kusche says, because no information can be found to explain them. "In several cases," he says, "important details of the incident, and in other cases, entire incidents, are fictional." [7]

During his research, he found nearly two hundred vessels that disappeared or were found abandoned between Northern Europe and the New England states since 1850. Some of the losses that occurred in other areas of the world, he discovered, were credited to the Triangle. [8]

"The most notable of these," Kusche says, "are the *Freya*, which was found abandoned in the Pacific Ocean in 1902, and the Globemaster that crashed near Ireland in 1951. If all the locations of 'Bermuda Triangle incidents' were plotted on a globe, it would be found that they had taken place in an area that included the Caribbean Sea, the Gulf of Mexico and most of the North Atlantic Ocean." [9]

Deliberate Lies

That so many incidents have been credited to the Triangle for sensationalism is understandable. But why are so many of the legends deliberate lies?

Partly for sensationalism. But not all.

Some theories are the result of, or are supported by, occult experiences. Such experiences, while containing just enough truth to seem palatable, cannot be trusted; they are riddled with lies, and their source is diabolical.

The Scripture warns about those who hold the "truth in unrighteousness," explaining that they have become "vain in their imaginations, and their foolish heart was darkened" because they "changed the truth of God into a lie." For this reason God has given "them over to a reprobate mind." [10]

We cite such experiences only to contrast fact and truth.

Spirit forces from the parallel world are the perpetrators of the mysterious. They are masters of illusion and half-truths. But could their passion for mystery be a cover for their real activity in the Triangle?

Their purpose is to set the stage for prophetic events and bring glamor to Lucifer's former kingdom, part of which is now beneath the sea.

Let's examine some of these lies:

GLOBEMASTER—A United States Air Force Globemaster was said to have disappeared on the northern edge of the Triangle en route to Ireland in March 1950.

The New York Times Index has no record of such an incident in 1950. But a *United Press International* story from London, carried in the March 30, 1951 issue of *The New York Times*, refers to a Globemaster that crashed at sea a few days earlier. The dispatch said the plane was blown to bits by an explosion, killing all fifty-three persons aboard. The plane had exploded and crashed at sea about 600 miles southwest of Ireland, the Air Force concluded.

Says Kusche:

> The disappearance . . . is too similar to the one mentioned in the Legend of the Bermuda Triangle not to be the same. It was a Globemaster, the incident occurred in March, and search headquarters were in Ireland, although the plane was not on a flight there, but to Britain. The loss occurred far away from the Bermuda Triangle, and it appeared to have been caused by an explosion.[11]

BILL VERITY—The Fort Lauderdale, Florida, ocean voyager was reported vanished in August 1969, north of Puerto Rico in a twenty-foot sailboat, *Brendan the Bold*.

He had set out from Ireland earlier that year in a craft he thought may be similar to one an Irish monk, Brendan the Bold, used to sail to Florida in A.D. 550.

The Coast Guard on August 21, 1969, issued a request for all ships to look out for the boat because it was dangerously near hurricane Debbie.

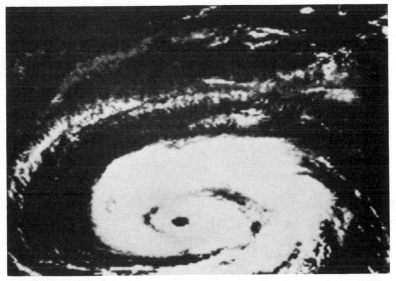

Hurricane Gladys, September 18, 1964, as seen by the weather satellite *Nimbus I* through an infrared device. Hurricanes and typhoons are spawned, respectively, in the Bermuda Triangle and the Devil's Sea. Photo: "Characteristics of Hurricanes," Miller, B.I., *Science*, Vol. 157, pp. 1389-1399, September, 1967.

"Nothing was heard until he arrived safely on San Salvador Island on September 14, saying that he had thought he was 'a gonner,'" Kusche reports.

"On November 30, 1973, I spoke by telephone with Verity. . . . He told me of his experience with hurricane Debbie and how he had been witness to five days of the finest display of wind, waves and lightning that anyone could ever wish to see, but that he was being reported as a victim of the Bermuda Triangle." [12]

WITCHCRAFT—Capt. Adrian Lonsdale of the Coast Guard says the *Witchcraft* is a perfect example of a combination of human error, mechanical failure and bad weather.

The twenty-three-foot cabin cruiser set out from Miami

on December 22, 1967, to view the city's Christmas lights. The owner radioed Miami Coast Guard a few hours later saying the *Witchcraft* was in trouble: she had a damaged propeller and was drifting near the harbor channel entrance in view of Miami. The Coast Guard was there in ten minutes, but there was no sign of the cruiser.

Lonsdale explains it this way:

> The night was windy, and one propeller was damaged, which reduced her speed. She had a Bermuda top—a canvas covering which acted like a sail. Between the action of the currents, the effect of the wind on her top, and her reduced speed, she was probably carried north toward Fort Lauderdale. From the sea, Lauderdale looks like Miami.
>
> When *Witchcraft* radioed that she was off Miami, she was actually off Lauderdale. We were looking in the wrong place. She must eventually have been carried out to sea, and that was the end of that.[13]

The wind was brisk enough to create white caps and waves were predicted to be as much as six feet high. It is easy to see how the cruiser could either be swept out to sea or swamped.

We have talked with Kusche since this article was published in *The Reader's Digest.* He has personally investigated this incident and discovered that parts of it were fabricated by one of the occult authors.

PIPER APACHE—This legend states that on a sunny day in April 1962, a twin-engine Apache radioed the Nassau control tower for guidance. The pilot was not able to determine his position, despite the excellent weather, implying he was flying in a dense fog.

Radio contact was lost after a few minutes of confusion. The legend states that the wing of the plane was found later that day about twenty miles from Nassau. The strangest element of the story is that the pilot was within sight of his destination when he radioed that he was lost.

Kusche says he searched every page of the *Nassau Daily Tribune* and the *Nassau Guardian* from January 1 through June 30, 1962, but found no mention of the incident. He also sent a letter to Nassau International Airport, telling about the incident and asking if officials there knew of any similar accident.

D.A.F. Ingraham, director of Civil Aviation at the airport, replied:

> "I refer to your letter, dated 11th March 1974. We have no record of the alleged disappearance of the aircraft you describe. Some of my staff and I have been with the Department of Civil Aviation since 1946. We have no recollection of the alleged occurrence to which you refer. I can only assume that it is a figment of someone's imagination.[14]

Natural Causes

In seeking to find legitimate answers to Triangle puzzles, researchers are discovering that the disappearances are not caused by invaders from outer or inner space, but by natural disturbances, mechanical failure and human error.

Let's examine some of these incidents:

TWO KC-135 STRATOTANKERS—Two of these stratotankers left Homestead Air Force Base, Florida, August 28, 1963, on a classified mission over the Atlantic. They made a routine report about noon, but were not heard from again.

There are two theories of how the "flying gas stations" could have vanished. One is a midair collision. The other, each plane had its own problems and went down separately.

Proponents of the mysterious rule out collision with the question, "Why was debris found in two separate areas almost two hundred miles apart?" They also rule out the possibility advanced by the second theory on the basis of logic.

They build their case for mystery by indicating officials are scratching their heads and will only say that "something very strange is going on out there." They advance their theory by implying that old-timers in the area are asking each other, "Who knows what evil lurks in the heart of the Bermuda Triangle?"

Richard F. Gerwig, chief of the Reporting and Documents Division of Norton Air Force Base where all Air Force accident reports are located, says a midair collision did occur between two tankers. The second sighting of debris, which gave rise to the mystery theory, was nothing more than trash and seaweed.[15]

FLIGHT 19—This is one of the most celebrated "disappearances" in the Triangle.

Lt. C.C. Taylor, commanding four student pilots and their crews, fourteen men in all, took off at 2:10 p.m., December 5, 1945, in clear weather from Fort Lauderdale. He led the flight of five navy Avenger torpedo bombers east over coastal waters on a navigational training run between Florida and the Bahamas.

About 3:40 p.m. Taylor radioed that his gyro and magnetic compasses were malfunctioning. He led his flight aimlessly east, then west and northeast over the ocean, trying to get his bearings by radio. Suddenly, Taylor gave orders to ditch. And shortly afterward, all contact was lost.

Two giant long-range seaplanes, Martin Mariners, were sent to search for Flight 19. Hours later, the seaplanes were ordered back to base because the wind had kicked up to thirty knots and visibility became limited. Only one Mariner landed, however.

The Navy and Coast Guard searched a 100,000-

Flight 19—TBM Avengers, similar to the five planes of Flight 19 that vanished with a total of five pilots and nine crew members on December 5, 1945, over the Bermuda Triangle. Photo: U.S. Navy.

square-mile area for days afterward with more than 100 surface craft and planes, but there was no trace of the Avengers or the seaplane. [16]

Flight 19 and the Mariner have since become lead actors in the spine-tingling mystery of the devil's playground, a mystery that has been fed by such statements as "They vanished as completely as if they'd flown to Mars. We don't know what the Hell's going on out there," [17] and the assumptions of writers seeking to create mystery.

One of these assumptions is that Lt. Taylor said over his radio, "Don't come after me . . . they look like they are from outer space."

The communication allegedly was picked up by a ham-radio operator. Art Ford, a reporter, author and lecturer, announced this "startling revelation" over a national TV program in 1974, saying he didn't give much credence to it at the time of the incident. But he later received corroboration in a transcript of the plane-to-tower messages. Ford noted the phrase, "Don't come after me" in the transcript, which he said was in common with that supplied by the short-wave radio operator.

Thus, the conclusion is drawn that there is other-world interference in the disappearance of Flight 19 and other Triangle incidents.

In reality, radio reception was so bad many of the messages between Flight 19 and the tower and search planes were garbled. To conclude anything more than "Don't come after me" in Taylor's message is pure speculation.

Testimony by Lt. Robert F. Cox, flight instructor at Fort Lauderdale Naval Air Station, clears up the mystery. He was flying around the field about 3:40 p.m. when he intercepted a radio message saying, "I don't know where we are. We must have got lost after that last turn."

Moments later he established radio communication with Taylor and gave him some instructions, closing the transmission with, "What is your present altitude? I will fly south and meet you." Taylor replied, "I know where I am now. I'm at 2,300 feet. *Don't come after me.*" [18]

Soon transmission faded, and Flight 19 was not heard from again.

Weather was a factor in the Avenger incident. While it had been clear when the planes took off, it deteriorated rapidly. Extreme turbulence and unsafe flying conditions were reported by search planes. Also, a ship in the area reported high winds and tremendous seas.

Taylor lost his bearings and failed or refused to switch to his emergency radio channel, which would have enabled

Martin Mariner—of the two Martin Mariners that were dispatched to search for Flight 19, only one returned. Photo: U.S. Navy.

him to pick up his position from shore stations. Panic probably set in, since the pilots were not experienced veterans, and their instructor was disoriented. The flight didn't disappear over a calm sea on a sunny afternoon, but on a dark, stormy night in a very rough sea.[19] Mystery solved!

SUPERFORTRESS—An American Superfortress bomber vanished one hundred miles off Bermuda in 1947. The legend itself speculates on what may have caused the disappearance: a tremendous current of air rising in a cumulonimbus cloud.

A cumulonimbus contains both downdrafts and updrafts invisible to radar, which can be in excess of two hundred miles an hour.

Coast Guard Capt. Marshall Phillips was flying in the

area in 1962 when he found himself in the grip of a sudden thunderstorm. Within seconds, his plane was violently thrust down, then up as though he had been fired from a slingshot. The thundercloud clawed fiercely at the plane's wings, trying to snap them off. When Phillips got clear, he discovered he was flying upside down at eight thousand feet.

Phillips believes the Superfortress must have flown into such a thunderstorm and been destroyed.[20]

AL SNIDER—In March 1948, the famous jockey and two friends went fishing near Sandy Key off the southern tip of Florida. They anchored their rented cabin cruiser in shallow water and rowed a short distance away in a skiff to fish. They didn't return to the cruiser. More than a thousand men and hundreds of planes and boats searched in vain for the missing men. The tender was found empty a few days later near a small island. But the men had vanished without a trace.

However, the *Miami Herald* reported a new wind velocity record for March had been set about the time the men were fishing. The gale had whipped up extremely heavy seas. [21]

THE SOUTHERN DISTRICTS—The freighter disappeared in the Straits of Florida in December 1954. The only trace of the sulphur-hauling ship and its crew of twenty-two was a life ring. There was no SOS.

Says Kusche:

The board of inquiry found that a north-northeast wind had blown in the area at the time the ship was thought to have sunk. Such a wind has a notorious reputation in the Gulf Stream area, as it blows against the northbound current and causes the stream to become choppy and violent, driving even the largest ships away from the strongest part of the current.[22]

A Boeing KB-50, like the one which, on January 8, 1962, disappeared between Langley Air Force Base, Virginia, and the Azores. Photo: Official U.S. Air Force Photo.

CONNEMARA IV—The yacht was found in September 1955, abandoned between the Bahamas and Bermuda. The victim of the mysterious Triangle? No.

The craft was caught in Hurricane Ione. Torrential rains, winds up to 182 miles an hour and waves up to 40 feet were reported.

Unexplained Mysteries

There are some phenomena, however, which do enhance the element of mystery.

TUG OF WAR—Capt. Don Henry, owner of a salvage company in Miami, was aboard a tug in 1966 headed for Fort Lauderdale from Puerto Rico. The tug, *Good News*, was towing a twenty-five-hundred-ton barge on a line a thousand feet behind.

They were over the Tongue of the Ocean; the weather was good; it was afternoon, and the sky was clear. Suddenly, the compass began spinning clockwise. Water seemed to be coming from all directions. There was no power in the tug's electric appliances and outlets, though the generators were still running.

Henry looked for the tow; it seemed to be covered by a cloud, and around it the waves were more choppy. He gunned the tug's motors, but something seemed to pull it back.

Henry says:

> Coming out of it was like coming out of a fog bank. When we came out, the towline was sticking out straight—like the Indian rope trick—with nothing visible at the end of it. I jumped to the main deck and pulled. The barge came out from the fog, but there was no fog any place else. In fact, I could see for eleven miles. In the foggy area where the tow should have been, the water was confused, although the waves were not big.[23]

WILD GOOSE—The sixty-five-foot shark-fishing boat was being towed in good weather south in the Tongue of the Ocean. As the vessels approached the southern section of the Tongue, where the submarine canyon emerges into a forty-mile-wide crater-like hole at its south end, the *Wild Goose* was seen by the crew of the towboat to go straight down "as if in a whirlpool." The crew cut the towline to keep from being drawn down with the *Wild Goose*.

C-119 FLYING BOXCAR—In early June 1965, a C-119 Flying Boxcar was lost in South Bahamian waters, about two hundred and eighty miles from Miami. It was en route to

Grand Turk with military parts. Newspaper accounts called its disappearance mysterious.[24] Although searchers combed two thousand square miles of the Atlantic, not a piece of wreckage or evidence of life was found.

Although the weather was fair, a number of reasons could have caused the crash—structural or engine failure, or an explosion. Waves were two to three feet high, and the wind was fifteen knots. The pilot would have had a problem ditching a disabled plane in those waves in the dark.

Were it not for another factor, we could credit this disappearance to the list of natural causes.

Gemini IV was in flight at the time of the plane's loss, during which Astronaut James McDivitt spotted a UFO with arms. To this day, according to the International UFO Bureau, the UFO has not been explained. McDivitt described the object as cylindrical, white, and with an "arm" sticking out. A number of theories have been offered, but none have satisfactorily explained the UFO.

Kusche contacted McDivitt about his sighting.

"I think it is important to realize that the letters UFO stand for Unidentified Flying Object," McDivitt replied. "The object which I saw remains unidentified. This does not mean it is, therefore, a spacecraft from some remote planet in the universe. It also doesn't mean that it isn't such a spacecraft. It only means that I saw something in flight which neither I nor anyone else was ever able to identify." [25]

The International UFO Bureau, in a series of articles, says it cannot help but wonder whether the C-119 had been captured by a UFO.[26]

This is pure speculation, of course, but we have already noted UFO activity in the Triangle and its parallel world significance. We cannot rule out the possibility of spirit-world interference any more than the probability that the C-119 was a victim of natural causes, though we do not agree that UFOs are from an alien planet. The fact remains: a UFO was sighted in the area at the time the plane disappeared, and both remain a mystery.

The Supernatural Is Involved

God's Word lifts the shroud of mystery from the phenomena of nature and their effects on man.

God, who created the elements, uses them for deliverance, spiritual lessons and judgments. Satan also uses the elements—for destruction.

Here's what the Word says:

WIND, LIGHTNING, EARTHQUAKES—The Lord sent a strong east wind to part the Red Sea for Moses (Exodus 14:21; Psa. 78:26), an east wind to bring locusts into Egypt (Exodus 10:11-13) and a west wind to drive them out (v. 19). He sent a wind, which brought quails from the sea (Num. 11:31).

He raised up a stormy wind (Psa. 147:18) and made the winds His messengers and the clouds His chariot (Psa. 104:3, 4).

The wind and the sea obey Christ (Mark 4:39; Matt. 8:27). And the winds are held back by angels (Rev. 7:1).

In the search for wisdom (Job 28), the question is asked: "Where can wisdom be found? And where is the place of understanding?"

The deep says, "It is not in me"; And the sea says, "It is not with me."

Abaddon and Death say, "With our ears we have heard a report of it."

God understands its way [wisdom]; And He knows its place. For He looks to the ends of the earth, And sees everything under the heavens.

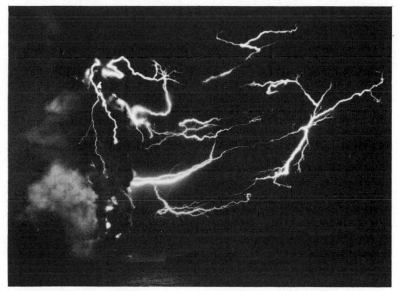

Displays of lightning. Bill Verity saw one of the finest displays of lightning over the Bermuda Triangle that he had ever seen. It occurred during a voyage in which he became another "claimed victim" of the Triangle. Photo: Sigurgeir Jonasson.

When He imparted weight to the wind, and meted out the waters by measure, when He set a *limit* for the rain, and a *course* for the thunderbolt, Then He saw it and declared it; He established it and also searched it out (Job 28:14; 22-27).

Job finally finds wisdom and the "place of understanding":

And to man He said, "Behold, the fear of the Lord, that is wisdom; And to depart from evil is understanding" (verse 28).

Since the "fear of the Lord is wisdom," then it stands to

79

reason that those in the nether world of departed spirits do not have wisdom (they are represented by the "sea," "deep," "Abaddon" and "Death").

Abaddon, who personifies destruction, is currently in Sheol-Hades. He is the diabolical king of the demon-centaurs that will be released during the fifth trumpet judgment of Revelation 9.

Job says God understands all about the wisdom of the elements of nature and that nothing happens by accident. He even sees a sparrow fall to the ground and knows the number of hairs on our heads (Matt. 10:29-30). God weighs the wind, measures the waters, limits the rain and sets the course for the thunderbolt.

The psalmist says whatever God pleases, He does:

In heaven and in earth, in the seas and in all deeps.
He causes the vapors to ascend from the ends of the earth;
Who makes lightnings for the rain;
Who brings forth the wind from his treasuries.[27]

When Elijah, the "prophet of thunder," was in a cave on Mount Horeb, he learned a lesson about the wind, earthquake and fire.

"Go forth, and stand on the mountain before the LORD."
And behold, the LORD was passing by! And a great and strong wind was rending the mountains and breaking in pieces the rocks before the LORD: *but* the LORD *was* not in the wind.

And after the wind an earthquake, *but* the LORD *was* not in the earthquake.

And after the earthquake a fire, *but* the LORD *was* not in the fire;

And after the fire a sound of a gentle blowing.[28]

Elijah was a prophet of judgment on the house of Ahab. He had seen God destroy Israel through many mighty acts and was despondent that God hadn't finished off the kingdom of Ahab and Jezebel.

Then God shows Elijah by the "gentle breath of God" that a God of judgment wants repentance.

The implication here is that the destructive forces of nature are for judgment in an attempt to warn man and thus to secure his salvation by bringing him back to "the fear of the Lord is the beginning of wisdom."

Even "Sheol" (Hebrew) means "a place of inquiry" to bring fear into the hearts of men that they would repent "by the storms of life" to the "gentle breeze of the Holy Spirit."

God doesn't enjoy judging His people, an attitude that Elijah was falling into as the sword of God. Before Elijah got too cynical, however, God showed him that He also was a "gentle blowing breeze."

This is the implication of Psa. 107:23-32, a portion of which is the text of this chapter. Men repented and gave thanks to the Lord for deliverance from the stormy sea, which He had caused to bring them to Himself.

Satan, according to Job 1-3, has similar power over the elements. Satan once was the "anointed cherub that covereth:" he was the steward of this planet and had control over the elements in the pre-Adamic Earth.

WATERSPOUTS—The psalmist refers to waterspouts in Psa. 42:7.

Deep calleth unto deep at the noise of thy waterspouts: all thy waves and thy billows are gone over me (KJV).

The Hebrew for deep is $t^e hom$, meaning a surging mass

81

of water, especially the deep, the main sea or the subterranean abyss.

Could this be one area of the abyss calling to another area, one gate calling to another gate?

The same word is used in Gen. 1:2 with the Luciferian Flood: "darkness on the face of the deep." It also is used with the Noahic Flood: "fountains of the deep broken up" (Gen. 7:11).

Job says Leviathan makes the deep to boil like a pot (Job 41:31). [29]

YELLOW HAZE—Warren and Betty Miller, missionary pilots, saw a yellowish haze during a recent flight near Cuba in the Triangle.[30]

Psa. 148:7 (KJV) gives an interesting correlation:

Praise the Lord from the earth, ye dragons (sea monsters), and all deeps:

Fire, and hail; snow, and vapour; stormy wind fulfilling his word.

Here the word for vapour is not the word used for clouds. It is used in only two other places in the Old Testament: in Gen. 19:28 of the *smoke* that went up from Sodom and Gomorrah, and in Psa. 119:83, where the psalmist says he was a "bottle in the *smoke.*"

Could there be a spiritual haze that is visible to some, which arises out of the Sheol-Hades compartment in the nether world?

When the lid is taken off the abyss in Rev. 9:2, it states

And he opened the bottomless pit; and smoke went up out of the pit, like the smoke of a great furnace; and the sun and the air were darkened by the smoke of the pit.

Joel prophesied of the time when God will "display wonders in the sky and on the earth, blood, fire and columns of smoke" (Joel 2:30).

Capt. Don Henry said the barge he had in tow seemed to be covered by a cloud, and the waves around it were more choppy than in other seas.

These incidents, when examined by Scripture, lead us to wonder about such inadvertent statements as: "flying into this mythical area is tantamount to sauntering through the *gates of hell.*"

People may scoff, but Jesus refers to the "gates of Hades" in Matt. 16:18, and Isa. 38:10 mentions the "gates of the grave" (Sheol). Note also the "gates of death" and the "doors of the shadow of death" in Job 38:17, Psa. 9:13 and 107:18.

MAGNETIC FIELD—Compasses have become erratic in the Triangle, a characteristic of many of the incidents. There are only two places in the world that compasses point true north—in the Bermuda Triangle and the Devil's Sea near Japan. All other places they point to magnetic north.

While it is a natural phenomenon, could it be that the departed spirits in the nether world look to the north in hopes of being released? North, the Bible says, is where Heaven is located. Note this passage:

But you said in your heart, I will ascend to heaven;
I will raise my throne above the stars of God, And I
will sit on the mount of assembly in the recesses of
the north (Isa. 14:13).

From Scripture we know that Sheol-Hades exists as an abode for departed spirits. But where?

The physical disturbances in the Bermuda Triangle and in the Devil's Sea give us a clue. They could be caused by spiritual contacts between God and Satan at the "gates of hell" in the continuing battle between good and evil in the parallel world.

Clairvoyants perceive this place, calling it the lost city Atlantis.

Hurricanes and typhoons are spawned there, much the same as the destructive forces in Job's day. According to Job 1, Satan has the authority to control the elements, causing death and destruction. It would appear that he's controlling the elements for destruction in the Triangle today.

It is comforting to note, however, that Satan was not allowed to touch Job's soul. Such it will be with Christians who venture into the Bermuda Triangle or the Devil's Sea. These disturbances will not affect their lives, for if they die, they will go to be with Christ.

Chapter 5

Mystery Solved

The path of life leads *upward for the wise, That he
may keep away from Sheol
below (Prov. 15:24).*

For thousands of years, the nether world has been an
abode for departed spirits.

The Bible calls it "Sheol" in the Old Testament and
"Hades" in the New Testament.[1] It is distinguished in Scripture from the *grave*, where the body goes at death.

The Hebrew word for *grave* in the Old Testament is
qeber. When a man dies, his body is placed in it. But his spirit
and soul go to Sheol-Hades.

Abode of Spirits

From Adam to the time of Christ, all departed spirits
went to Sheol-Hades, which was divided into compartments. One was a place of torment where the wicked went.
Another—called Abraham's bosom and Paradise (Luke
16:22; 23:43)—was a place of comfort and hope where the
righteous went at death.

The Bible says there was a great gulf separating these
compartments, so that none could pass between (Luke
16:26).

It wasn't possible for the righteous who had died before Christ to go to Heaven because Christ had not yet shed His blood in atonement for man's sin. They had to wait until Christ came.

Some Bible scholars call them "prisoners of hope," taking their thoughts from Isa. 14:17, which says that Satan "did not let his prisoners go home" (RSV).

Sheol-Hades is depicted as a prison with bars. Note these passages:

. . . He (Christ) went and preached unto the spirits in prison (I Pet. 3:19 KJV).

They shall go down to the bars of the pit . . . (Job 17:16 KJV).

At His death, Christ went "into the heart of the earth" (Matt. 12:40) to preach to these spirits in prison (I Pet. 3:18-20; 4:6), and take them home to Heaven.

Paradise Transferred

The Bible doesn't explain all that happened when Jesus went to Sheol-Hades between His death and resurrection. But we do know He released the departed spirits of Abraham's bosom and took them into the presence of God in Heaven (Eph. 4:8-11).

Sheol-Hades always is *down* in Scripture, while Heaven always is *up*. When Jesus was on the cross, He said to the penitent thief, "This day thou shalt be with me in Paradise." At that moment, Paradise or Abraham's bosom was still a *down* compartment of Sheol-Hades. Biblical references to Paradise after the resurrection, however, place it *up* in God's Holy City, (Rev. 2:7; 22:14), called Heaven.

Other Compartments

Apparently there are several compartments in this nether world prison.

Besides the section where wicked spirits await judg-

ment and the one-time Abraham's bosom, another called
Tartarus is mentioned in II Pet. 2:4, where the angels who
intermarried with the daughters of men are confined.[2] This
intermarriage between fallen angels and humanity brought
the flood of purging and sent the pre-Noahic race into Tartarus to await special judgment.

In Rev. 9:14, 15, four angels came out of the river
Euphrates after they had been loosed. Is there another
compartment of Sheol-Hades under the river?

The locust-scorpion centaurs of the Apocalypse are
locked up in the bottomless pit and have Abaddon as their
king (Rev. 9:1-5, 11). Is this also a compartment?

The demonic beast, which possesses the Antichrist of
the Apocalypse, is loosed from the bottomless pit (Rev. 11:7;
17:8).[3] He also is said to *come out of the sea* (Rev. 13:1).[4]

We must say here, however, that whether all of these
come out of the same compartment or are locked up in
different places is open for speculation. But there is strong
indication in biblical and extra-biblical experience to support
this theory.

Glimpse of the Nether World

The testimony of Lorne F. Fox, a missionary evangelist
for a major denomination, is an example of such extra-
biblical experience.

An angel at his side, he was taken in spirit *down* into the
nether world where he was first permitted to see the fate of a
lost soul. Here are excerpts from his account:

"At first, everything was clothed in total darkness, and
then after a time there began to be faint, weird lights and
shadows, like a flickering firelight, which gradually became
brighter.

"At this point, the atmosphere, which had been warm,
became stifling, finally almost unbearable, and then the descent ceased for a few moments.

"The lost soul was just below, and by now it was possible to discern that he was joined by a weird creature, which arose from the lower regions. It was a demon, sent from Hell to take that soul by force on the remainder of its downward journey.

"The descent began again. Far below us, things now began to take a definite form. There appeared a huge orb or sphere, which was bathed in flames of liquid fire. At closer proximity, the sphere was so large that it was impossible to begin to see around it. This had been the source of the mysterious firelight.

"Finally, the descent stopped as we came close against this vast orb. I saw a fierce struggle for just a moment between the lost soul and that demon, and suddenly, with a wild shriek the soul was plummeted headlong into the wall of fire that covered this huge sphere.

"The angel placed his hand over my eyes and said, 'Be not afraid.' I felt suddenly as though I was being plummeted through space at a great speed. Then the motion ceased, and when the angel removed his hand from my eyes, I found that I was on the inside of a different realm. I heard the voices of lost souls lifted in cries, shrieks and curses. Somehow, I knew fully that those were the realms which we speak of here on Earth as Hell.

"The angel led me into a vast open arena. The ceiling and walls were ornate . . . beautiful, if that is possible, in a hideous sort of manner. The floor was paved with blackest ebony. In the center of this vast place stood a huge black throne, trimmed in jade green.

"At first glimpse, I saw that the throne was empty. Ornate black steps led down from its crest. At the bottom of the steps, I saw someone standing, his back to me. . . ." [5]

Moments later, still under escort, Fox was taken to another realm where he saw countless lost souls engaged in a variety of tormenting activities.

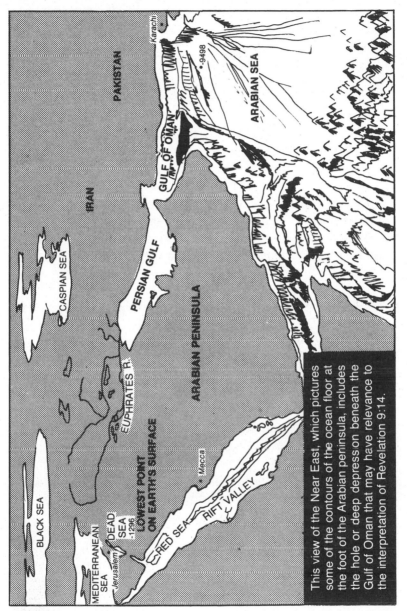

This view of the Near East, which pictures some of the contours of the ocean floor at the foot of the Arabian peninsula, includes the hole or deep depression beneath the Gulf of Oman that may have relevance to the interpretation of Revelation 9:14.

Marietta Davis, a young woman who lived in the mid 1880s, saw two regions of the nether world and returned to describe it.

The first she depicts as a realm of illusion. The second, a realm of vice. Here are some excerpts from her accounts:

"Suddenly a sable veil of nether night appeared . . . I fell as one precipitated from some dizzy height. The moving shadow of a more desolate abyss arose like clouds in dense masses of tempestuous gloom; and as I *descended*, the ever-accumulating weight of darkness pressed more fearfully upon me.

"At length a nether plain that seemed boundless was imaged upon my sight, which, at a little distance, appeared to be covered with the sparkling semblance of vegetation. Luminous appearances, like waving trees, with resplendent foliage, and flowers and fruits of crystal and of gold were visible in every direction.

"As I advanced, I walked as upon scorpions, and trod as amid living embers. The trees that seemed to wave about me were fiery exhalations, and their blossoms the sparklings and the burnings of unremitting flames. Each object I approached by contact created agony.

"The phosphorescent glare that surrounded the various objects burned the eye that looked upon them. The fruit burned the hand that plucked and the lips that received it. The gathered flowers had emitted a burning exhalation, whose fetid and noisome odor caused excruciating pain."

Miss Davis continues her narrative, describing the residents of this compartment and their woes. Then she is led to a second sphere, "where I could perceive nothing but lonely space."

She describes the darkness as more dense in this region.

"A vast arena opened to my view, in which I saw at one glance every imaginable species of vice, forms and fashions of human society, government, clans and all the varied phases and forms of worships, originating in every kind of religion, from the heathen to fashionable church-going people, who heartlessly worship.

"As this scene opened, I heard a voice from far above me saying, 'Marietta, fear not; but behold a pandemonium, where congregate the self-deceived; hopers in false philosophy, together with the despisers of God . . . where hypocrisy unveils its hideous shape, and religious mockery speaks in its own language. . . ." [6]

What she saw in this region closely resembles sights Lorne Fox witnessed. Did Miss Davis and Fox visit the same realm?

Popular consensus is that Sheol-Hades has only one compartment for departed spirits since the transfer of Paradise to Heaven. But could there be many varying degrees of torment in this region?

Entrances to the Nether World

To the ancient Greeks, bottomless pit meant "depths of original time," "the primitive ocean" and "floods of water." In Luke 8:31, demons asked Christ not to send them into the "deep" (Greek: *abussos*—depths of the sea).

This same pit is used in Revelation as the prison of the underground (Rev. 20:7; 20:2). It has gates (Matt. 16:18; Isa. 38:10), with keys to it (Rev. 1:18; 9:1, 2), and smoke rising out of it (Rev. 9:2).

We ask, could the disturbances in the Bermuda Triangle and the Devil's Sea have some connection with the entrances to the biblical Sheol-Hades? Are its gates being bombarded by internal and external spiritual forces, releasing tremendous physical forces in nature?

There could be two gates, or possibly twelve if Ivan Sanderson's theory is correct.

The two would be in the Triangle and the Devil's Sea.

The gates are located in the two deepest places under the sea, known as the Mariana Trench off Guam at 36,198 feet and the Puerto Rico Trench at 27,500 feet.

The Bible never mentions gate in the singular when referring to Sheol-Hades, always in the plural. If we bored a hole parallel to the equator straight through the world from the Bermuda Triangle, it would emerge in the Devil's Sea. The Bible reference to gates could mean they are side by side in one location. But, if we accept the two chasms on either side of the Earth, it could be two separate gates.

Sanderson's theory is that there are twelve vortices (whirlpools) of electromagnetic aberrations and these are at 72° intervals around the world, making five in the northern hemisphere and five in the southern with two at the poles.

The New Jerusalem, the heavenly city of Revelation 21, has twelve gates (Rev. 21:12). Could it be that the city of departed spirits also has twelve gates? One of these gates, Sanderson says, is at the mouth of the Euphrates River. It is here that the four demon angels are loosed to lead the 200 million infernal horsemen into battle during the period of the Apocalypse (Rev. 9:14).

The Scripture refers to the "gates of Hell" (Sheol) in Matt. 16:18, the "gates of the grave" (Sheol) in Isa. 38:10, the "gates of death" and the "doors of the shadow of death" in Job 38:17, Psa. 9:13, 107:18.

Not only does the Scripture refer to the gates as an entrance to the nether world, but also behind the gates is a corridor that leads into the underground chamber. Lorne Fox, when describing his visit to the nether world, said, "At first, everything was clothed in total darkness, and then after a time there began to be faint, weird lights and shadows, like a flickering firelight, which gradually became brighter."

Clairvoyant Dykshoorn says the Bermuda Triangle "is

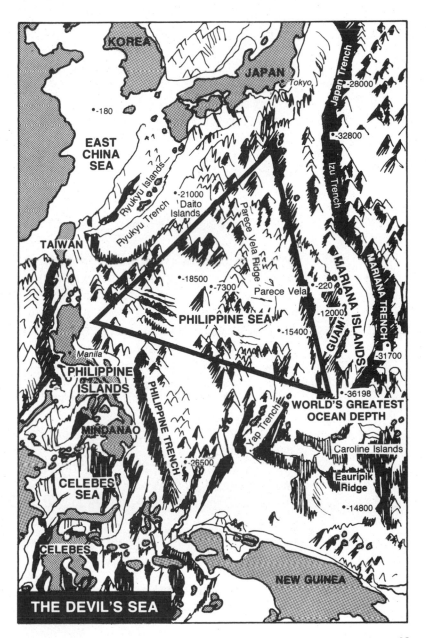

THE DEVIL'S SEA

a giant vortex or whirlpool that originates from *a hole* in the floor of the ocean." While this is a deduction from a cultist, it deserves notice, for Satan is aware of its existence. Scriptures corroborate the hole-corridor theory. Note: "hole of the pit" (Isa. 51:1), "grave's mouth" (Psa. 141:7) and "pit shut her mouth upon me" (Psa. 69:15).

Jacques Bergier, a French scientist and Fellow of the Royal Society of Arts, also suggests there are secret doors to the Earth, phenomenal passageways to other worlds within the visible Earth.

He tells of seven energy levels, called dwipas, which are worlds like ours. At least one of the dwipas is inhabited, he says.

"On it there lives the King of the World, who safeguards that which is essential to humanity, its spiritual aspirations," he says. "It is possible to go to the city of the King of the World and come back. It is also possible to encounter on Earth its messengers just returning. And lastly, it is possible to receive a teaching that originates from this city." [7]

The Bible, of course, doesn't support his dwipa theory, but it does have some interesting parallels. For example, it calls Satan the "god of this world" (II Cor. 4:4), and it describes Satanic influence on human spiritual aspirations. The Bible also supports the idea of travel to and from the spiritual and physical realms.

Demonic beings, of course, are the Bible's definition of Bergier's dwipa messengers. And that it is possible to receive teaching from the spirit world is not only indicated by Scripture, it is evident in all the cultic religions of the world.

Bergier believes the frontier between Earth and other Earths, though invisible, is easily crossed, which could account for occult experiences.

He concludes, "If our Earth is a place of passage, there must be *doors* that lead to the unknown. We have not the

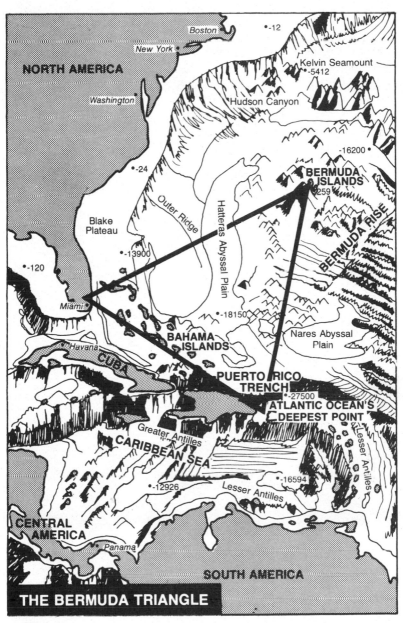

THE BERMUDA TRIANGLE

slightest idea how a door is created. Once it is created, however, such a door makes possible accidental passages, and this could explain the appearance of things and people." [8]

Bergier says the sites suspected of harboring secret doors are distinguished by the disruption of gravity and terrestrial magnetism; visions by visitors at the site and enigmatic disappearances. He places one of the doors in the Bermuda Triangle.

Chapter 6

Abyss under the Sea

The departed spirits tremble under the waters and their inhabitants.

Naked is Sheol before Him and Abaddon has no covering (Job 26:5-6).

Man has only one frontier left.

Earth's lands have been explored, its wildernesses conquered and its resources harnessed.

Science has conquered the smallest of Earth's molecules, and electronic microscopes that can magnify a silver dollar to the size of New York's Central Park have observed the smallest building block of biology—the DNA molecule—out of which all life is pre-determined.[1]

Man also has walked on the moon and is sending space probes to other planets in the universe. But he has another frontier to explore. One with many mysteries.

Frontier of Mysteries

The ocean is a great thermal engine. Most of the sun's energy passes virtually unimpeded throughout the atmosphere into the ocean where it is absorbed and transformed. Nearly a third of the solar energy reaching the Earth's surface goes to evaporate sea water. The thermal inertia of the sea, the circulation of the water and the geographic distribution of ocean and land profoundly influence our planet's weather and climate.[2]

The ocean has locked many secrets in its depths, such as the living fossils recently found that were supposedly extinct. And other species of marine life have been found, bringing their number to more than two hundred thousand with new finds on every oceanographic expedition.

What other secrets will man find in the coming years?

Sound in the ocean travels much farther than in the air. An explosion of a one-pound block of dynamite in the air can be heard for about a half mile. Such an explosion at mid-depths in the ocean can be heard for many thousands of miles.[3]

What will man hear as he listens to the sounds of the inner Earth from the depths of the Bermuda Triangle and the Devil's Sea in coming years?

The fluid character of water on our planet is the miracle that makes life possible. But because the oceans fill the low places of Earth, they are the ultimate sink of ever increasing human and industrial wastes.

Undersea Civilization

Yes, the sea has many mysteries, and it serves many purposes. Not only is it the depository of man's wastes and the thermal engine of the world, the sea is a cover for a vast underworld civilization consisting of the departed spirits of the human race and of fallen angels.

As ancient man believed his body was buried in a pit, so he also believed his spirits went into the abysses of the Earth under the sea.

God's book, the Bible, bears this out. It calls this underworld civilization Sheol-Hades.

The following verses relate to Sheol-Hades, indicating that its gates or entrances are under the sea and that there is a corridor called "the bottomless pit" or "abyss," which leads from the surface of the planet to the Sheol-Hades nether world beneath the sea:

1. Gerhard Kittel says in his *Theological Dictionary of the New Testament:*

   Sheol-Hades signifies the dark (Job 10:21) "realm of the dead" which is set beneath the ocean (26:5), and which consigns all men indiscriminately (Psa. 89:48) behind its portals. . . .[4]

2. Dr. Finis Dake says in reference to Job 26:5-6:

   The place of the departed spirits of giants and ordinary wicked men is beneath the oceans and under the earth.[5]

   Dake bases his conclusion on three translations of that passage:

   The Septuagint: Are giants going to rise up from beneath the water and the places near its neighborhood?

   Moffatt translation: Before Him the primeval giants writhe, under the ocean in their prison; the underworld lies open to His eyes.

Fenton translation: The Rephaim, themselves, were destroyed. And rest under the seas.

3. The departed spirits tremble under the waters and their inhabitants.

Naked is Sheol before Him

And Abaddon has no covering (Job 26:5-6).

This is the theme verse of this chapter. The majority of Bible commentators agree that "under the waters" refers to the sea. Here is a direct reference placing Sheol under the sea and naming one of its inhabitants, Abaddon.

4. Because you have said, "We have made a covenant with death,
And with Sheol we have made a pact,
The overwhelming scourge will not reach us when it passes by,
For we have made falsehood our refuge and we have concealed ourselves with deception."

And your covenant with death shall be canceled,
And your pact with Sheol shall not stand;
When the overwhelming scourge passes through,
Then you become its trampling *place* (Isa. 28:15, 18).

Isaiah is speaking to wicked rulers in Jerusalem, who say they have made a "covenant with death," "a pact with Sheol;" therefore, they say, the overwhelming scourge will not reach us when it passes by. But verses 16 and 17 state that He is laying a "cornerstone in Zion," referring to the coming Messiah. He is going to make justice "the measuring line" and righteousness "the level."

Isaiah goes on to say, "hail shall sweep away the refuge of lies and the waters shall overflow the secret place" (verse 17).

Isaiah was referring to the coming Babylonian invasion when they would burn Jerusalem to the ground. This was the overwhelming scourge that would punish these wicked rulers.

A secondary interpretation is the use of scourge with Sheol. A scourge is a whip used to beat a criminal, and it is used this way in verse 18 when God says, "Your pact with Sheol shall not stand; when the overwhelming scourge (whip) passes through." But the word "scourge" in verse 15 is not the same Hebrew word; here it means "an oar of a boat" as used for whipping up the waves. Some translations use the word "flood" in this verse, describing the "overflowing waters" over the Sheol compartment. Rephrasing verse 15, it would read:

And with Sheol we have made a pact. The overwhelming flood will not reach us when it passes by.

5. On its ruin all the birds of the heavens will dwell. And all the beasts of the field will be on its *fallen* branches in order that all the trees by the waters may not be exalted in their stature, nor set their top among the clouds, nor their well-watered mighty ones stand *erect* in their height.

For they have all been given over to death, to the earth beneath, among the sons of men, with those who go down to the pit. Thus says the Lord GOD, "On the day when it went down to Sheol I caused lamentations; I closed the deep over it and held back its rivers. And *its* many waters were stopped up, and I made Lebanon mourn for it, and all the trees of the field wilted away on account of it.

I made the nations quake at the sound of its fall
when I made it go down to Sheol with those who go
down to the pit; and all the well-watered trees of
Eden, the choicest and best of Lebanon, were com-
forted in the earth beneath. They also went down
with it to Sheol to those who were slain by the
sword; and those who were its strength lived under
its shade among the nations" (Ezek. 31:13-17).

Ezekiel is referring to the great nation of Assyria (verse
31:3), and likens it to a cedar tree. The many rivers that
flowed through Assyria made it green and prosperous.
However, the Lord was going to stop these "waters" and
give them the "waters" of the "deep."

On the day when it went down to Sheol . . . I
closed the deep over it. . . .

The "deep" is the subterranean waters at great depths
(see appendix, chapter 2). The Lord stopped the rivers so
that this "cedar tree" (nation of Assyria) wilted away and fell
under the judgment of the waters of Sheol. Again the Bible
correlates Sheol with waters.

6.   They will bring you down to the pit. And you will
      die the death of those who are slain in the heart of
      the seas (Ezek. 28:8).

Judgment is pronounced upon the Prince of Tyre. Again
"pit" is associated with "heart of the seas."

7.   Then Jonah prayed to the Lord his God from the
      stomach of the fish, and he said, I called out of my
      distress to the Lord, and He answered me. I cried
      for help from the depth of Sheol; Thou didst hear
      my voice. For Thou hadst cast me into the deep,
      Into the heart of the seas, And the current engulfed

me. All Thy breakers and billows passed over me. So I said, "I have been expelled from Thy sight." Nevertheless I will look again toward Thy holy temple.

Water encompassed me to the *very* soul, The great deep engulfed me, Weeds were wrapped around my head. I descended to the roots of the mountains. The earth with its bars *was* around me forever, But Thou hast brought up my life from the pit, O LORD my God (Jonah 2:1-6).

While this is descriptive of the sea and fish, it has in the mind of Jonah all the descriptions of Sheol. Words like "depth of Sheol," "the deep," "heart of the seas," "current engulfed me," "breakers and billows passed over me," "water encompassed me," "deep engulfed me," "weeds were wrapped around my head," "roots of the mountains," "earth with its bars," "brought up my life from the pit," are all descriptive of the abysses of Sheol-Hades.

8.   He will again have compassion on us; He will tread our iniquities underfoot. Yes, Thou wilt cast all their sins into the depths of the sea (Micah 7:19).

This verse speaks of Christ's burial for our sins. God says our sins have been cast into the depths of the sea. Christ died on the cross to atone for our sins. He was buried and for three days went to Sheol-Hades (I Pet. 3:19). Our sins not only were nailed to the cross but carried into the "depths of the sea."

The deepest place in the sea is the Mariana Trench about 6.8 miles down off Guam. The Empire State Building in New York is 1,248 feet high. Twenty-nine Empire State Buildings could be stacked on top of each other in this ocean depth, and there would be still twenty-eight feet to spare!

Mount Everest, the world's highest mountain, is 29,141 feet high. If Mount Everest was put in this deepest ocean depth, there would be 7,057 feet of water above its peak!

There are eight tons of pressure per square inch in the ocean's deepest point.[6] In God's ocean of pardon, there is the pressure of His divine love—all the love shown by Christ in Gethsemane, at Calvary, and at His burial and resurrection. Once our sins are cast into the sea of His pardon, the pressure of His love keeps them in the depths of the past!

9.   And Jesus asked him, "What is your name?" And he said, "Legion"; for many demons had entered him. And they were entreating Him not to command them to depart into the abyss. Now there was a herd of many swine feeding there on the mountain; and *the demons* entreated Him to permit them to enter the swine.

And He gave them permission. And the demons came out from the man and entered the swine; and the herd rushed down the steep bank into the lake, and were drowned (Luke 8:30-33).

The word "Legion" comes from the Roman legions, which numbered from four thousand to six thousand men. Whether there were this many demons possessing the man is open for conjecture. The Bible does say, however, that "many demons had entered him."

The demons asked Christ not to send them into the "abyss." Demons know of the "abyss" and, as we have said in earlier chapters, they glamorize it by making it their hereditary birthplace.

This "abyss" is the same word used in Rev. 9:1 and 20:1 (*bottomless pit* in the King James Version). This is the New Testament counterpart for the Old Testament "deep" in Gen. 1:2 (see appendix, chapter 2).

Christ granted the demons their request and sent them into a herd of swine feeding nearby. Here an interesting thing happens—the swine run down a steep bank into the lake and are drowned. If these demons were the disembodied spirits of the pre-Adamic race, they had experienced drowning before in the flood at Lucifer's fall. Hence, they knew that by rushing this herd of swine into the lake, they could gain their freedom to reenter humans rather than animals.

10. And he stood on the sand of the seashore.

> And I saw a beast coming up out of the sea, having ten horns and seven heads, and on his horns *were* ten diadems, and on his heads *were* blasphemous names (Rev. 13:1).

According to many Bible commentators, this "beast" is the end-time Antichrist. The "beast" represents three things:

a. He is a demon prince who presently is locked up in the "abyss" and will be released in the end-time Tribulation (Rev. 11:7). This is the same beast here that is coming up out of the sea from the "abyss." (Some believe this demon prince is the revived "Prince of Greece," mentioned in Dan. 10:20.)

b. He is a mortal man and receives power from the dragon in the end-time (II Thess. 2:3-12; Rev. 13:4-10). This mortal man is possessed by the demon prince which comes up out of the abyss in Rev. 11:7.

c. He also is a kingdom, the eighth and last kingdom before the second coming of Christ in which he is the sole head (Rev. 17:11).

Why Under the Sea?

Sheol-Hades is under the sea because of the two great destructive floods. Water covered the Earth in both the Luciferian and Noahic judgments. The inhabitants—the primeval giants, the Nephilim, and humanity—were drowned and covered in a deluge of water by which the Lord cleansed His planet to prepare it for future generations. Concerning the flood of Noah, the Bible says:

> Then the LORD saw that the wickedness of man was great on the earth, and that every intent of the thoughts of his heart was only evil continually. And the LORD was sorry that He had made man on the earth, and He was grieved in His heart. And the LORD said, "I will blot out man whom I have created from the face of the land, from man to animals to creeping things and to birds of the sky; for I am sorry that I have made them . . . And behold, I, even I am bringing the flood of water upon the earth, to destroy all flesh in which is the breath of life, from under heaven; everything that is on the earth shall perish" (Gen. 6:5-7, 17).

The Nephilim were destroyed by the Noahic Flood (Gen. 6:4). After the intermarriage of His fallen angels with the daughters of Adam's seed, God was sorry He had made mankind. This corruption of pure Adamic stock is one of the reasons for the beginning of the Sheol-Hades nether world.

There is a special judgment awaiting these angels, as II Pet. 2:4 says:

> God did not spare angels when they sinned, but cast them into hell and committed them to pits of

darkness, reserved for judgment; and did not spare the ancient world, but preserved Noah, a preacher of righteousness, with seven others, when He brought a flood upon the world of the ungodly. . . .

The word for hell here is "Tartarus," the lowest compartment of Sheol-Hades. This is the only time this word is used in the Bible, and in Greek writings Tartarus was believed to be a place lower in the Earth than Hades, where lived the Titans (giants), the primeval deities who were supposed to be the first children of the Earth, even older than the Greek gods. These deities, according to Greek mythology, were cast into Tartarus when they lost their war with the head god, Zeus.[7]

This is the first historical mention in the Bible of a nether world compartment. Tartarus came into existence for the Nephilim during the time of Noah. It is probably out of this lowest compartment in Sheol-Hades that many of the demonic beings are released during the tribulation.

We have no evidence that any fallen angels were put into Sheol-Hades before the Noahic Flood. The angels who fell with Lucifer could have remained loose until the Noahic Flood. This is speculation, of course, but we know that many fallen angels still are not confined; they are free to roam the Earth under Satan's control. It will be during the tribulation that the ones chained in Tartarus will rejoin their comrades on Earth to prepare for the battle of Armageddon (Rev. 9). It is during this seven-year period that "all hell breaks loose."

Until the resurrection of Christ, all departed spirits were kept in Sheol-Hades.

In the previous chapter, we saw how this nether region was divided into two areas. One was called Abraham's bosom, or Paradise, and was for the righteous. The unrighteous were kept in an area apart from Paradise. The sections were separated a great distance so that residents of either side could not cross to the other, the Bible says.

After the resurrection, Christ took those in Paradise and "when He ascended on high, He (Christ) led captive a host of captives" (Eph. 4:8) into Heaven. Paradise is there now; it is no longer in Sheol-Hades. These Old Testament saints He presented to the Father, having redeemed them by His death on the cross.

Since the resurrection and the ascension of Christ, every person who believes in Christ's death, burial and resurrection and accepts Christ's atonement for his sins goes *up* into Paradise to be with the Lord (II Cor. 12:4; I Cor. 15:1-11). All who reject Christ's death in atonement for their sins (II Thess. 1:7-9), go *down* into the Sheol-Hades compartment, which is constantly being enlarged (Isa. 5:14). They await the resurrection of their mortal bodies to stand trial before the Great White Throne at the end of this age (Rev. 20:11-15).

Lucifer's Legions

The Bible defines the compartment under the sea as Sheol-Hades. The occult calls it a "lost civilization."

The occult is aware that life exists under the sea. Through reincarnation occultists say humanity originated from a former civilization on the lost continent Atlantis. Clairvoyants and those under hypnosis, such as Edgar Cayce, perceived such a place.

How is this done? Not through reincarnation, but through demon possession.

Demonic spirits seek, by inhabiting people, to gain recognition in the physical world and to glamorize their pasts by making themselves and those they possess seem to be one and the same person.

It is only when people do not honor God and His Word that they leave themselves open for this invasion.

Demons who inhabit people are Lucifer's legions. They are set in array against God's forces (Mark 5:9). They have ranks and positions—rulers—powers—world forces of this darkness—spiritual forces of wickedness in heavenly places (Eph. 6:12; Col. 2:15).

Some Bible commentators believe there are two kinds of fallen creatures under Lucifer's control:

Disembodied spirits—spirits that once had bodies, but lost them in the fall of Lucifer. They are the pre-Adamic race.

Demons—angels who fell with Lucifer, possibly one third of God's angels (Rev. 12:4).[8]

The disembodied spirits, according to these commentators, were beings who lived before Adam; their bodies were destroyed during the Luciferian Flood. These were released into the atmosphere but remained under the control of the devil to this present age.

They are called "evil spirits" (I Sam. 16:14; Luke 7:21, 8:2; Acts 19:12-16), and could be the lowest order of the Satanic forces. If these are the spirits of the pre-Adamic race, which Lucifer ruled over, this would be the reason for the animalistic, carnal attitudes of people infested with these porno-spirits.

Also, it would give the truth about reincarnation. It is not the entities and personalities of people who lived in the past whom the demons are impersonating, for their spirits and souls are kept in Sheol-Hades until the resurrection. But it is the evil disembodied spirits of those who lived under Lucifer's reign before Adam that are infesting the human race.

These spirits inhabit the bodies of people today and

have a knowledge of past people, places and things. They can recite these facts while the inhabited person is under hypnosis. They also can describe the lost continent Atlantis, their hereditary birthplace, which was destroyed "in a day and a night" (Plato's *Dialogues*).

Nether World Gates under the Sea

The gates or entrances to Sheol-Hades are under the sea. We've shown in previous chapters that the physical and natural disturbances at these entrances come from the spiritual warfare being waged there for the souls of humanity.

Ivan Sanderson suggests that there are twelve "vortices" or electromagnetic aberrations around the world. He established a network of twelve "anomalies" at seventy-two-degree intervals.[9]

As already mentioned, two of these correspond to the Bermuda Triangle in the Atlantic and the Devil's Sea off Japan and Guam.

Such terms as "Devil's Triangle," "Devil's Sea" and "Hoodoo Sea," have been in the conversation of mariners for years. It hasn't been until the last few years that the great depths under these mysterious areas have been known.

The Puerto Rican Trench lies under the Bermuda or Devil's Triangle at 27,500 feet and the Mariana Trench lies under the Devil's Sea off the Island of Guam at 36,198 feet.

The Earth's crust varies from sixteen to forty-four miles thick and is the thinnest under the oceans, especially the Atlantic and Indian Oceans where it is only sixteen to twenty-two miles thick.

Again, geographically speaking, the gates to Sheol with the shortest corridors to inner earth would be under the seas, particularly at its greatest depths.

Another of Sanderson's gates is at the mouth of the Persian Gulf into which the Euphrates River empties. It is at this mouth that ocean bottom topographical maps show a deep hole.

Note the following passage of Scripture:

> And the sixth angel sounded, and I heard a voice from the four horns of the golden altar which is before God, one saying to the sixth angel who had the trumpet, "Release the four angels who are bound at the great river Euphrates" (Rev. 9:13-14).

Could the deep hole at the mouth of the Persian Gulf be the one from which the four angels are loosed from the abyss to lead 200 million horsemen from the East into the battle of Armageddon?

Ancient Dungeons

In Old Testament times criminals were punished by being placed in pits in the ground. Some pits were wet and damp abandoned wells.

King Zedekiah put Jeremiah into one of these for prophesying the overthrow of Jerusalem by the Babylonians. In this misty, muddy dungeon he would have died except for the pleas of his friend, Ebedmelech, to the king (Jer. 38:6-13).

Others who were cast into pits for punishment were Joseph, by his brothers (a waterless pit, Gen. 37:24), and Daniel, who was taken up out of the lion's den (Dan. 6:23). The Psalmist in his prayer of deliverance from his foes says:

> Deliver me from the mire, and do not let me sink;
> May I be delivered from my foes, and from the deep waters. May the flood of water not overflow me, And may the deep not swallow me up, And may the pit not shut its mouth on me (Psa. 69:14-15).

Boring a hole in the ground and burying family clans in

SHEOL-HADES COMPARTMENT

In Old Testament Sheol which is used 65x was a divided compartment with the saints going to Abraham's Bosom and the unrighteous going to Hades. Since the death, burial, and resurrection of Christ—the saints go to Heaven with Christ.

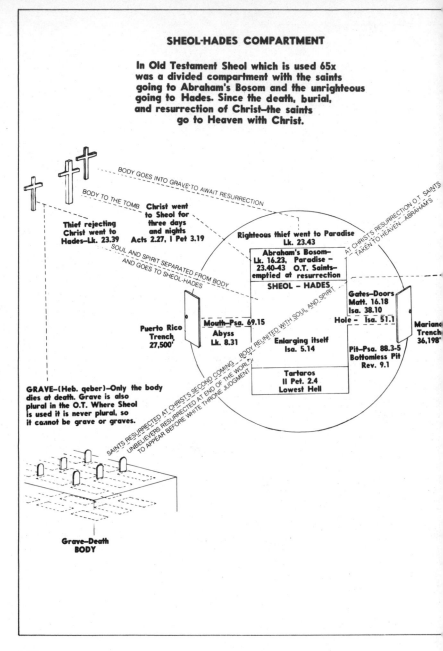

BODY GOES INTO GRAVE TO AWAIT RESURRECTION

BODY TO THE TOMB

Christ went to Sheol for three days and nights Acts 2.27, I Pet 3.19

Thief rejecting Christ went to Hades—Lk. 23.39

SOUL AND SPIRIT SEPARATED FROM BODY AND GOES TO SHEOL-HADES

Righteous thief went to Paradise Lk. 23.43

AT CHRIST'S RESURRECTION O T SAINTS TAKEN TO HEAVEN—ABRAHAM'S

Abraham's Bosom— Lk. 16.23, Paradise — 23.40-43 O.T. Saints— emptied at resurrection

SHEOL - HADES

Gates—Doors Matt. 16.18 Isa. 38.10

Hole – Isa. 51.1

Puerto Rico Trench 27,500'

Mouth—Psa. 69.15 Abyss Lk. 8.31

Enlarging itself Isa. 5.14

Pit—Psa. 88.3-5 Bottomless Pit Rev. 9.1

Mariane Trench 36,198'

Tartaros II Pet. 2.4 Lowest Hell

GRAVE—(Heb. qeber)—Only the body dies at death. Grave is also plural in the O.T. Where Sheol is used it is never plural, so it cannot be grave or graves.

SAINTS RESURRECTED AT CHRIST'S SECOND COMING— BODY REUNITED WITH SOUL AND SPIRIT

UNBELIEVERS RESURRECTED AT END OF THE WORLD TO APPEAR BEFORE WHITE THRONE JUDGMENT

Grave—Death BODY

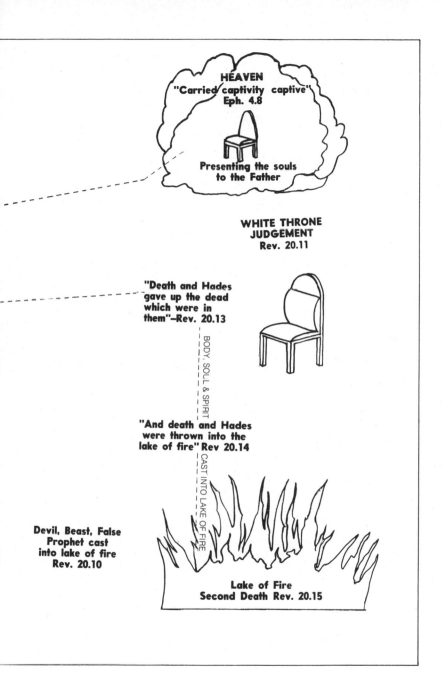

HEAVEN
"Carried captivity captive"
Eph. 4.8

Presenting the souls
to the Father

WHITE THRONE
JUDGEMENT
Rev. 20.11

"Death and Hades
gave up the dead
which were in
them"—Rev. 20.13

BODY, SOUL & SPIRIT

"And death and Hades
were thrown into the
lake of fire" Rev 20.14

CAST INTO LAKE OF FIRE

Devil, Beast, False
Prophet cast
into lake of fire
Rev. 20.10

Lake of Fire
Second Death Rev. 20.15

the sides of the pit at different elevations was another ancient custom. (See appendix.)

Ezekiel uses this custom to explain to Israel how God was going to bury and destroy His enemies:

> Assyria is there [in the pit] and all her company; her graves are round about her . . . whose graves are set in the remotest parts of the pit, and her company is round about her grave.

> Elam is there and all her multitude around her grave.

> Meshech-Tubal and all their multitude are there; its graves surround them (Ezek. 32:22, 24, 26).

In this passage Ezekiel likens these underground mausoleums to Sheol-Hades. For as the *bodies* are buried in underground pits, likewise the departed *spirits* go into a lower pit, the nether world under the oceans. Here is a definite analogy between the burial holes for family clans and the nations who forget God. Verse 21 in this section says:

> The strong among the mighty ones shall speak of him and his helpers from the midst of Sheol, "They have gone down, they lie still . . ." (Ezek. 32:21).

In Ezek. 32:17-30 the word "pit" is used five times. This is the Hebrew word *bor* whose root meaning came from "a hole in the ground for cooking." This word also is translated "dungeon," "well," "cistern," and "fountain."

This "pit" or hole in the ancient's mind was the entrance into the nether parts of the Earth where Sheol is located (Ezek. 32:18-24).

In summary, this is a picture of the nations who reject the Lord (Psa. 9:17). Each nation then has its own burial hole, their bodies being deposited in the pit and their spirits descending further down into the nether parts of the Earth—to Sheol-Hades. (For the word "pit" used in other places with "Sheol," see the appendix.)

In Isa. 14:15, "Sheol" and "pit" occur together again, this time in references to the future when Lucifer, the devil, will be bound for a thousand years. John the Revelator describes this occasion at the end of the tribulation period:

> And I saw an angel coming down from heaven, having the key of the abyss and a great chain in his hand. And he laid hold of the dragon, the serpent of old, who is the devil and Satan, and bound him for a thousand years, and threw him into the abyss, and shut it and sealed it over him, so that he should not deceive the nations any longer . . . (Rev. 20:1-3).

The New Testament word "abyss" (bottomless pit) and the Old Testament "pit" are similar.

This "abyss" is the entrance-corridor into the nether world of Sheol. It is during the thousand-year period, when Christ reigns on Earth, that the Sheol-Hades compartment will serve its final purpose. During this time, all of the forces of darkness will be chained beneath the seas, including the devil and other spirits that have rejected the Lord and His Christ.

Occultists have been prophesying for years that the lost continent Atlantis will rise again, proving a lost civilization is under the sea. What if God, before the second coming of Christ, and the thousand-year period, would open the doors to Sheol-Hades for all to see?

It is interesting to note again that the root meaning of "Sheol" is "a place where men inquire," "an inpenetrable hiding place." In light of this, how man's curiosity has been aroused over the Bermuda Triangle!

Chapter 7

Leviathan—
King of the Sea

In that day the LORD *will
punish Leviathan the fleeing serpent, with His fierce
and great and mighty
sword, even Leviathan the
twisted serpent; and He
will kill the dragon who
lives in the sea (Isa. 27:1).*

Are sea monsters real or imaginary? Are they spiritual
entities from a civilization under the sea who assume the
physical appearances of monsters? Are these creatures of
the deep responsible for some of the unexplainable disappearances in the Bermuda Triangle and the Devil's Sea?

Or, are they merely grotesque, but innocent, mutations
of prehistoric creatures living in the deep?

The conjecture of some occultists is that sea monsters
are real and that from time to time they pluck down into
their abysmal abodes vessels sailing the high seas.

There have been many sightings of sea monsters in the

vicinity of the Bermuda Triangle. Could the occultists be right? If so, what can we expect from these creatures in the future?

Sea Monsters of the Bible

In chapter 3 we noted two outstanding indications of the entrance to Sheol-Hades in the Bermuda Triangle—the migratory spot of the North American and European eels and the giant vortex of the floating Sargasso seaweed.

We turn now to Scripture to see what it says about sea creatures and their relationship to Sheol-Hades and its entrances.

The prophet Amos, in describing remote places where a fugitive may hide from God, says:

> Though they dig into Sheol . . . and though they conceal themselves from My sight on the floor of the sea, from there I will command the serpent and it will bite them (Amos 9:2, 3).

Note the association of Sheol with the floor of the sea in Job 41. But this is not the only reference to the word serpent where it is associated with the sea. Three other Hebrew words refer to a serpentine sea creature (see appendix):

LEVIATHAN—described as a frightening monster of the seas in Job 41. This name occurs five times in the Old Testament, always as an evil entity allied with Satan. He is called king of the sea.

RAHAB—called a fleeing sea serpent in Job 26:12, 13. In chapter 6, "Abyss Under the Sea," we showed how Job 26:5, 6 describes Sheol-Hades as under the sea and names one of its demonic inhabitants, Abaddon. Verse 13 identifies another of Satan's demons as Rahab. This creature is free.

In Psa. 87:4, Rahab is likened to Egypt, which was drowned in the Red Sea, thereby overcoming and crushing the evil entity over those waters.

118

This name occurs four times. It should not be confused, however, with Rahab the harlot, who was spared by Joshua in Jericho.

DRAGON—the common Hebrew word for any large sea creature. This word refers to Leviathan in Isa. 27:1 and to Rahab as Egypt in Isa. 51:9.

Dragon occurs fourteen times in the Old Testament and is translated as "sea monster," "serpent" or "dragon." It refers to any large sea or marine creature that is monstrous or hideous—good or bad—including the "sea monsters" God created in Gen. 1:21. (The smaller creatures of the sea are called "living creatures" and "fish" as in Gen. 1:21, 26).

Spiritual Bodies

In chapter 1 we showed how UFOs are evil entities in tangible form. We also explained that the reason there has been no physical evidence of their existence is because they are spiritual craft; they can pass in and out of physical, visual perception at will.

We now ask:

Are sea monsters spiritual entities from a civilization under the sea who assume the physical appearance of monsters?

Do supernatural beings exist who are not spirits, but flesh? Or who can assume the form of flesh? The answer is yes!

The Apostle Paul speaks of various bodily shapes and forms—some heavenly and some earthly—in I Cor. 15:35-41. Note verse 39:

> All flesh is not the same flesh, but there is one flesh
> of men, and another flesh of beasts, another flesh of
> birds and another of fish.

In this context, Paul is discussing the resurrection of the human body by the power of Christ's resurrection. The

119

human body will be similar to the one Christ had after his resurrection, he says.

Jesus was able to walk into a room with the doors and windows closed after He rose from the dead. Yet He was not spirit. He had a body of flesh and bone. Jesus said, "handle me, and see; for a spirit hath not flesh and bones, as ye see me have" (Luke 24:36-39).

We know from Scripture and experience that angelic beings can assume human form, often appearing in the cultural dress of the times. And the Scripture instructs us to entertain strangers because in so doing we might be entertaining angels unawares (Heb. 13:2).

Does Satan have spiritual forms for his angels like God does for his?

What other beings exist in this world or under its seas who, though of a different dimension, can assume the appearance or form of flesh? The form of man or beast . . . or of sea monster!

We are witnessing incredible signs of Christ's second coming. And UFOs, legendary sea monsters—possibly even the "Big Foot" creature of the Pacific Northwest and the giant birds sighted recently along the Rio Grande River in Southern Texas—and the phenomenal rise of the occult are evidences that the world is becoming more and more demonized as the time of Christ's coming draws near.

Phantoms of the Deep

Though many sightings are frauds or pranksters' jokes, we can't discount the testimonies of all who say they have seen monsters, for their statements have held up under lie detector tests.

And many sea monsters have been reported in the vicinity of the Bermuda Triangle. For example:

GIANT JELLYFISH—seen by Richard Winer, writer of *The Devil's Triangle,* while doing underwater filming for

General Electric south of Bermuda in water more than four thousand feet deep. The appearance of this huge sea creature was "like a giant jellyfish," Winer says, "and was over fifty feet in diameter, perfectly round with a color of deep purple. Its outer perimeter was pulsating." [1]

The creature frightened Winer and his safety diver, Pat Boatwright, as it moved slowly toward them. They quickly started to ascend, and as they did they saw the giant creature descending into the blackening depths.

GLOUCESTER SEA SERPENT—In August 1917 a sea serpent was sighted off of Cape Ann, Mass. by many persons which caused an investigation from the Boston Society of Naturalists. Members of the society reportedly came within 139 yards of the monster, which they estimated to be ninety feet long, and clocked its swimming speed at thirty miles per hour. Shortly after the visit by the society, it vanished from the sea. [2]

GIANT SQUID—may be as large as the giant sea serpents. The size of these giant squid can be calculated by occasional skeletal remains that have been recovered and by disk marks on the backs of whales where the suction marks of the squid's tentacles have taken away the pigment from whales' hides while leaving the outline. These could have been caused by titanic struggles in the depths of the oceans. [3]

OTHER SIGHTINGS—In *The Bermuda Triangle* Berlitz says many reliable observers have sketched or described sea creatures, which resemble the structure of the pliocens monosaurus or ichthyosaurus. Many believe these sea creatures are still alive in the abyssal deeps. [4]

The fossils of these dinosaurian reptiles were first found at Lymie Regis on the south coast of England, which was a popular sea bathing resort in the nineteenth century.

Mrs. Anning, a widow, and her daughter, Mary, made a living by selling to tourists these fossil ammonities (ancient round, flat sea shells), which they found on the beaches along the coast.

One day, in 1821, they inadvertently found a cliff below Lymie that was full of giant sea fossils—a complete specimen of the monosaurus, a sea reptile like an armoured fish; the first examples of the bird-like pterodactyl and the plesiosaur. Today, these are in the Kensington Science Museum along with a picture of Mary Anning, their discoverer.

Some scientists believe that some of these prehistoric creatures could still exist today in the ocean's depths. They cite the recent findings of the coelacanth off the Comoro Islands in the Indian Ocean, which was thought by many to have become extinct millions of years ago. If the coelacanth managed to survive so long undetected, why not the plesiosaur? [5]

Even Jules Verne could not create such a hideous creature as the flying pterodactyl. When the French scientist, Baron Culvier, reconstructed this flying monster from the remains discovered by Mary Anning, he wrote that the picture of it in its living form "will be so extraordinary that it seems the result of a diseased imagination rather than forces of nature." [6]

Almost a century later, Conan Doyle, in *The Lost World*, wrote about these creatures. He said, "the face of the creature was like the wildest gargoyle [a grotesque figure] that the imagination of a mad medieval builder could have conceived. . . . It was the devil of our childhood." [7]

Doyle, a medical man of his day, had rejected the doctrine of hell that terrified his Edinburgh childhood. For him the devil was as much a product of the diseased imagination as the gargoyles or this creature from the lost world.

That such creatures did exist is a matter of record, and scientists like Doyle are discovering there is a hell on this

Earth, and its cast of hideous creatures is acting out the last drama.

Fresh Water Sea Monsters

LOCH NESS MONSTER—Frank Searle keeps a cold, lonely vigil on the placid waters of Loch Ness, but he vows to continue his watch until he proves that the monster lurking below really does exist.

The latest time Searle claims he spotted the creature he affectionately calls "Nessie," was April 22, 1975.

"Two American girls and some visitors from Ayr were with me," he says, "when this big back broke the surface out toward the middle of the lake."

"They were extremely fortunate," the bachelor said; "you could hang around here for years and never catch a glimpse like that."

Six years ago, Searle abandoned his job as a fruit stand manager in London to make camp along the Loch Ness shoreline in Scotland and be ever alert for another sighting of the monster.

"I've been on the lookout for twenty thousand hours now," the British ex-paratrooper said. "Logged twenty-four sightings and six pictures." [8]

At 1 a.m. August 8, 1972, contact was made with "Nessie" with sonar by four researchers, reports MITs 1976 March/April *Technology Review.* As they made initial sonar contact with a large submerged object moving under their boat, the authors recall:

> If primitive instincts are any sign, there was something ominous in the loch that night; the hair went up on the backs of [our] necks.

About forty minutes later salmon began breaking the water's surface, apparently trying to escape two objects, clearly discerned by sonar, swimming about twelve feet apart.

In 1975 the researchers returned to take more photographs. Indistinct as they are, certain conclusions have been made about the nature of the "Nessie." The creatures are about twenty feet long, including a slender neck. The weight may be more than a ton. Long projections extend from the top of the head which some scientists speculate could be breathing snorkels.[9]

Continued research is planned, and the *New York Times* co-sponsored a scientific expedition in the summer of 1976, costing about seventy-five thousand dollars.[10]

"Nessie" started her world-wide acclaim on April 14, 1933. Before then, she was considered a legend.

Dr. Barron, editor of the local newspaper, *Inverness Courier*, is said to have remarked, "We can't go on calling this thing a creature. If it's as big as people say it is, then it must be a real monster."

So in the press, the mysterious animal became the Loch Ness monster, named after the Scottish lake by that name.

Since that first headline in 1933, monster mania has been underway with three thousand claimed sightings of "Nessie," one hundred and fifty of them published in detail.

Though public interest has been stirred since the 1930s, the "Nessie" legend goes back hundreds of years. The first reported sighting of a monster is given in an eighth century biography of Saint Columba, the Irish poet who converted the Picts, written a century after his death by his compatriot, Adamnan. One of the chapters is entitled "Of the Driving Away of a Certain Water Monster by Virtue of the Prayer of the Holy Man."

The incident took place about A.D. 565.

At another time, again when the holy man was staying for some days in the Province of the Picts, he found it necessary to cross the river Ness. When he came to the bank, he sees some of the local people burying an unfortunate fellow, whom—so those burying him claimed—some aquatic monster had shortly before snatched while he was swimming and viciously bitten. The corpse had been rescued by some boatmen armed with grappling hooks. The holy man orders one of his companions to swim out and bring over a cable moored on the other side. Hearing and obeying the command, Lugne Mocumin without delay takes off his clothes except his loin cloth and casts himself into the water. But the monster, perceiving the surface of the water disturbed by the swimmer, suddenly comes up and moves towards him as he was crossing in the middle of the stream, and rushed up with a great roar and open mouth.

The holy man seeing it . . . commanded the ferocious monster saying "Go thou no further nor touch the man. Go back at once." Then on hearing this word of the saint the monster was terrified and fled away again more quickly than if it had been dragged on by ropes. . . .[11]

Peter Costello, who records this incident in his recent book, *In Search of Lake Monsters*, believes it is a true story, but slightly exaggerated.[12]

HIGHLAND WATER HORSES OF SCOTLAND—For many years there have been folk tales of sightings of water monsters in the lochs of Scotland. One such creature is mentioned in a poem by James Goff. In 1807 he wrote, "in some places of the highlands of Scotland, the inhabitants are still in continual terror of an imaginary being called the water-horse." [13]

Traditions say that the early inhabitants of the land

sacrificed to these water-horse deities by casting valuables and animals to them. To this day many of these articles can be found on the bottom of the lochs.

POOKA AND PIAST OF IRELAND—Lake monsters, says naturalist Robert Lloyd Praeger, "are an accepted part of Irish zoology." [14]

Irish historian Dr. P.W. Joyce observed that "legends of aquatic monsters are very ancient among the Irish people." [15] He shows that many places in Ireland have been named after water-horses called by the name of the Pooka and the Piast.

One such creature was seen in 1921 by Thady Byrne. He describes the creature this way:

> It was black, and as big as a greyhound, but it was like a cat. It had long bristles cocking out from each side of its jaws, but not a braid of hair upon its tail. It had a great jowl on it, like a bulldog, and a great wide chest and shoulders, and he tapered away to his tail. You'd hear him barking at night in the woods, and the bark was like the squeal of a seagull. [16]

THE STORSJO OF SWEDEN—Lake Storsjo is the deepest lake in Sweden. Between 1820 and 1898 about twenty-two trustworthy witnesses reported spotting this sea creature named after Lake Storsjo.

A farmer in 1820 claimed the animal had followed his boat near Funas at the south end of the lake.

In 1830, a house painter who saw it called it "the Storsjo Leviathan."

As recently as the summer of 1965, *The Scandinavian Times* reported a new outbreak of the sightings. After giving details, the magazine said tourists were flocking to the lake in hopes of seeing the animal. [17]

SLIMEY SLIM OF THE UNITED STATES—In Lake Payette in Idaho is the legend of Slimey Slim. The animal was first seen on July 2, 1941, by Thomas L. Rodgers, the auditor of a respectable Boise firm. He described Slimey this way:

> The serpent was about fifty feet long and going five miles an hour with a sort of undulating movement . . . His head, which resembles that of a snub-nosed crocodile, was eight inches above the water.

Slimey Slim, plus scores of other citings, are listed in the book *In Search of Lake Monsters* by Costello.

Costello, who did research for years accumulating data around the world, believes many of these accounts are true—that they are prehistoric creatures that haven't yet been found, but will be in the near future.

Other sightings include the Ogopogo of Canada, the Patagonian plesiosaur of South America and the dragon of the Ishtar Gate of western Asia. All of these show a universal belief in water and sea monsters.

Both Sir Richard Owen in 1848 and Sir Arthur Keither in 1934 classed the sea serpent and the Loch Ness monster with ghosts and ghouls rather than animals of flesh and blood. Sir Arthur was quite emphatic on this point:

> The only kind of being whose existence is testified to by scores of witnesses and which never reaches the dissecting table, belongs to the world of spirits . . . I have come to the conclusion that the existence or non-existence of the Loch Ness Monster is a problem not for zoologists but for psychologists. [19]

Costello goes on to say "that the only other writer who seems seriously to have considered the idea that monsters might be psychic phenomena was the late T.C. Lethbridge." [20]

We partly agree that these sightings, if not frauds, are personifications of evil entities, which the Bible calls rulers, powers, world forces of this darkness and spiritual forces of wickedness (Eph. 6:12), some of which rule the seas and waterways.

Some of these spirits can assume extinct marine forms, which were real physical creatures at one time that could possibly have been destroyed in the Luciferian or Noahic floods.

Two of these evil heads are called Leviathan and Rahab in the Bible.

Killer Submarines

Even as the United States and Russia are battling for the supremacy of the seas, so are the forces of Satan battling for control of the seas on behalf of the residents of Sheol-Hades.

Just as the nations name their submarines according to different classes, such as "Poseidon" and "Polaris," so also two of Satan's sea patrols are named in the Bible—the "Leviathan" and "Rahab" classes.

Though many Bible commentators make Leviathan and Rahab synonymous with the devil, it is our thesis that they are separate marine entities under his control. The reasons are this:

1. Leviathan and Rahab are never related to the devil in the eight times they are mentioned.[21]

2. Personal pronouns and titles are used for these creatures.

    "He is King [Leviathan] over all the sons of pride" (Job 41:34).

    (Personal pronouns are used sixty-three times in Job 41 to describe a real creature.)

Rahab's helpers crouch beneath God (Job 9:13).

3. Leviathan was associated with a living marine creature that was familiar to the Hebrew mind in their day:

"There is the sea, great and broad, in which are swarms without number, animals both small and great and Leviathan, which thou hast formed to sport in it" (Psa. 104:25-26). See also Job 3:8.

4. In the last days the Lord will destroy Leviathan "who *lives* in the sea" (Isa. 27:1), "in that day" refers to end time. Read Isa. 26:21; 27:2-13).

This cannot refer to the devil because he is "prince and power of the air" and lives in his kingdom of this world, which comprises both land and sea (Eph. 2:2).

The first two mentions of Leviathan are found in Job 3:8, 41. Rahab is listed for the first two times in Job 9:13 and 26:12.

Sea monsters sighted around the world are generally described to look like the ancient plesiosaur, a dragon-like marine creature that could have existed before Noah.

The description of Leviathan in Job 41 is similar to this ancient dragon of the seas. Leviathan had a tongue, nose, jaw, skin, head, teeth, scales, eyes, mouth, breath, neck, and heart.

Since no living physical creature like this is known to exist today, though it has been sighted by reliable sources, we contend that such sea monsters are like UFOs, evil entities in tangible form.

UFOs are included in the "wonders in the sky above," while sea monsters are among the "signs on the earth beneath" heralding the second coming of Christ (Act. 2:17, 19).

Several interesting conclusions to incidents in the Bermuda Triangle are related to Leviathan:

LIGHTS AND TORCHES—When Columbus first sailed through the Triangle, he recorded in his diary that he saw "lights and burning torches silhouetted on the water." His men thought they were nearing land, but as they sailed toward the lights, they disappeared; it was many more days before they found land.[21]

Listen to the Bible's account of Satan's patrol over the gates of Sheol-Hades by Leviathan.

His sneezes flash forth light (Job 41:18).

Out of his mouth go burning torches, sparks of fire leap forth (Job 41:19).

Prayer brought many to the new world where they could enjoy religious freedom. Was there a battle over the Bermuda Triangle between God's angels and Leviathan for the safe passage to a new land?

Many mariners have seen lights and torches in this area through the years. The "white water" in the Triangle was the last light from the Earth that the astronauts could see on their way into space.

SMOKE—Capt. Don Henry encountered a heavy fog that engulfed the barge he was towing. In his words, "coming out of it was like coming out of a fog bank." This was a strange phenomenon since "there was no fog any place else." [22]

Warren and Betty Miller, missionary pilots, saw a yellowish haze on the sea during one of their flights over the Triangle. It was during this time that they encountered erratic compass gyration and a strange glow in the aircraft.

Again, listen to the Psalmist describe the characteristics of sea monsters.

Praise the LORD from the earth, ye dragons [sea-

monsters] and all deeps: Fire, and hail; snow, and
vapour; stormy wind fulfilling his word (Psa. 148:7,
8 KJV).

We mentioned earlier that the word for vapour is not
the Hebrew word for cloud, but for smoke. It is used this
way in Gen. 19:28, describing a burning spot of
destruction—Sodom and Gomorrah.

Now, note this characteristic of Leviathan:

Out of his nostrils smoke goes forth, as from a
boiling pot and burning rushes (Job 41:20).

PHYSICAL DISTURBANCES—We have seen earlier that
hurricanes, which are spawned in the Triangle, are caused
by spiritual warfare between the forces of evil and good. One
of Satan's rulers, Leviathan, is said to make "depths boil like
a pot" and "the sea like a jar of ointment [that is shaken up
and foaming]" (Job 41:31).

EXORCISM—Rev. and Mrs. Gerald Stahly had a
specialized ministry of exorcism when they pastored a
church in Santa Barbara, California, several years ago.
Along with some of their faithful members, they would fast
and pray for the deliverance of those who were troubled or
possessed by demons. Some individuals were brought to
them from many miles away.

The Stahlys were amazed that when they asked the
demons to identify themselves they would sometimes reply,
"Leviathan."

The name was never suggested by the exorcists, and
the possessed person seldom had previous knowledge of the
term Leviathan.

When the name of Jesus was invoked, many were released from the power of this evil entity. Even as Rahab has
helpers, Leviathan also can control many evil entities.

As the end-time coming of Christ approaches, because men refuse to acknowledge God and his Word, the Lord will allow Satan to exhibit more miracles than ever before.

Occultism is on the increase; Eastern religions are making vast inroads into the Western world, the greatest stronghold of Christianity. Many are forecasting the end of the church age with the advance of science and the metaphysical religions of works.

Apart from a recent upswing in attendance among fundamental churches, there has been a great exodus from the old-line Christian denominations. There is a vacuum in the Western world's youth; the stage is being set for great end-time supernatural miracles:

> The one whose coming is in accord with the activity of Satan, with all power and signs and false wonders, and with all the deception of wickedness for those who perish, because they did not receive the love of truth so as to be saved. And for this reason God will send them a deluding influence so that they might believe what is false (II Thess. 2:9-11).

If you hear of UFOs, giant birds, sea monsters or the wonders of psychics, know they are not from or of God.

> For false Christs and false prophets will arise and show signs and wonders, so as to mislead, if possible even the elect (Matt. 24:24).

G.H. Pember, in his book *Earth's Earliest Ages,* cited seven things that led to the Noahic Flood and said these seven conditions will exist in the world just before the second coming of Christ.

"This, many would quickly reply, is certainly an event which has not yet startled our age, strange as our experiences may be," he wrote at the turn of the century. "We have

Phil Thompson and his partner came across this mysterious footprint while hunting near Coos Bay, Oregon, in 1976. The impression measured seventeen inches in length by seven inches in width. Photo: UPI tele-photo.

still something at least to wait for before the completion of that fatal circle of influences which ruined the old world. But a diligent comparison of Scripture with the things that are now taking place among us will give a very different impression and induce a strong conviction that the advanced hosts of this last terrible foe have already crossed our borders.

"For it is no longer possible to deny the supernatural character of the apostasy called Spiritualism, which is spreading through the world with unexampled rapidity, and which attracts its votaries, and retains them within its grasp, solely by continual exhibitions of the miraculous." [23]

God is not the only one who is supernatural: so is Satan. Let us have the staff of Moses and Aaron in our hands today. The "magicians of Egypt" might be able to turn their staffs into serpents, but God's staffs will consume them by the breath of *His mouth* (Exod. 7:8-13).

Chapter 8

Abaddon— King of the Abyss

> *They have as king over them, the angel of the abyss; his name in Hebrew is Abaddon, and in the Greek he has the name Apollyon (Rev. 9:11).*

Leviathan and Rahab roam the seas and fight for the control of the entrances of Sheol-Hades. As we said in the last chapter, their shapes and forms are similar to the ancient sea creatures of the Mesozoic period—the plesiosaurs.

During the coming tribulation period, these evil forces will finally gain release of their comrades below, including their king—Abaddon.

The Final Battle

North of Jerusalem and east of Mount Carmel lies the Plain of Esdraelon. It is on this plain that Bible authorities believe the battle of Armageddon will be fought.

In this final climactic battle just before the return of

Christ, the Lord allows Satan to regroup by releasing two demon orders from Sheol-Hades:
1. The scorpion-centaurs (Rev. 9:1-11).
2. The two-hundred-million demon horsemen (Rev. 9:13-21).

In both of these groups we see the shapes of horses, the favorite animal of the former world kingdom of Poseidon-Lucifer.

As we have noted in previous chapters, horses were sacrificed and honored during Lucifer's former reign upon Earth. Also, the horse latitudes were so named because ancient mariners jettisoned their war horses into the ocean to conserve their water. These latitudes run through the Triangle, where the scorpion-centaurs, whose appearance is like a horse and scorpion, are turned loose during the tribulation to torment men for five months (Rev. 9:5).

What this torment is, the Bible doesn't say, except the curse of this plague is that "men will seek death and will not find it; and they will long to die and death flees from them" (Rev. 9:6).

The Revelator's Vision

The Apostle John records this vision in A.D. 94 on the Isle of Patmos during the reign of the Roman Emperor Domitian. He was banished as an exile to this small, remote, barren island in the Aegean Sea from Ephesus, where he had served as the overseer to the seven churches of Asia Minor (Revelation 2, 3).

In interpreting this difficult section in Revelation 9, as well as any other portion of Scripture, the general rule is to take the Bible literally instead of spiritually. The rule observed is:

Take the Bible literally wherein it is at all possible;
if symbolic, figurative or typical language is used,
then look for the literal truth it intends to convey.[1]

Listen to John's words in this light:

> And the fifth angel sounded, and I saw a star from
> heaven which had fallen to the earth; and the key of
> the bottomless pit was given to him. And he opened
> the bottomless pit; and smoke went up out of the
> pit, *like* the smoke of a great furnace; and the sun
> and the air were darkened by the smoke of the pit.
> And out of the smoke came forth *locusts* upon the
> earth; and power was given them, as scorpions of
> the earth have power (Rev. 9:1-3).

Note that these are called locusts—one of man's most
dreaded destroyers of crops and vegetation. Then John,
giving the description of these locusts, uses the words "as"
and "like." These locusts which come up out of the bottomless pit in the midst of smoke had these likenesses:

1. Their *appearances* are *like horses* prepared for battle (9:7).
2. On their *heads*, crowns *like gold* (9:7).
3. *Faces* like faces of *men* (9:7).
4. *Hair like* hair of *women* (9:8).
5. *Teeth like* the teeth of *lions* (9:8).
6. *Breastplates like* breastplates of *iron* (9:9).
7. *Sound of wings like* the sound of *chariots* (9:9).
8. *Tails and stings like scorpions* (9:10).

Note that these are all spiritual forms and likenesses.
John calls them locusts because of the *destructive force* they
bring upon the Earth.

Finally, they have a king over them—Abaddon, the
angel of the abyss (Rev. 9:11).

The Destroyer

The devil is the chief destroyer (John 10:10), and all of
his hosts have the spirit of their leader. Some have said that

Abaddon is another title for the devil. It is our thesis that Abaddon is currently locked up in Sheol-Hades (see appendix). Also, that he is one of Lucifer's former rulers in his kingdom before Adam.

He is locked up along with the scorpion-centaurs and the demon horsemen possibly for the same reason that other of his hosts are presently in the nether world.

Peter says:

> God did not spare the angels when they sinned, but cast them into hell and committed them to pits of darkness, reserved for judgment (II Pet. 2:4).

And Jude says:

> And angels who did not keep their own domain, but abandoned their proper abode, He has kept in eternal bounds under darkness for the judgment of the great day (Jude 6).

When the Bible says Abaddon is the angel of the abyss, it does not say in Rev. 9:11 that he is confined there. This is concluded from the following five Old Testament Scriptures:

1. The departed spirits tremble under the waters and their inhabitants. Naked is Sheol before Him and Abaddon has no covering (Job 26:5-6).

This Scripture not only shows that Sheol is under the sea, but names one of its inhabitants, Abaddon, who is naked with no covering before the Lord.

The Lord is aware of this personage under the sea. Abaddon is translated "a place of destruction" in some Bible versions.

Speaking of the place of Sheol, however, as we take all the Scriptures dealing with Abaddon we will find that the Bible is speaking of a real demon entity.

There are many words in the Hebrew language for destruction which are used throughout the Old Testament. When Abaddon is used, the writers are speaking of a real person whose character is to destroy.

2. Sheol and Abaddon lie open before the LORD, How much more the hearts of men (Prov. 15:11).

Abaddon is associated again with Sheol, a person and a place that is not hidden from the eyes of the Lord, though men are not aware of it.

3. Sheol and Abaddon are never satisfied, Nor are the eyes of man ever satisfied (Prov. 27:20).

As Jesus said, "for the gate is wide, and the way broad that leads to destruction, and many are those who enter by it" (Matt. 7:13). As it is with Sheol, Abaddon and the eyes of man, "they are never satisfied," for "Sheol is being enlarged" (Isa. 5:14).

4. Wilt Thou perform wonders for the dead? Will the departed spirits rise *and* praise Thee? [Selah.] Will Thy lovingkindness be declared in the grave, Thy faithfulness in the place of destruction? (Psa. 88:10-11).

The phrase "Thy faithfulness in the place of destruction" can be translated "Thy faithfulness in *Abaddon.*" The same word is used in the original.

These are contrasting virtues, for "the dead won't wonder anymore" and "departed spirits [Nephilim—fallen rebel angels] won't rise and praise the Lord" nor is "there any lovingkindness in the grave" much more "faithfulness in Abaddon," the angel of destruction.

Again, notice how all of these describe death and the nether world.

139

5. And to man He said, "Behold, the fear of the Lord, that is wisdom; And to depart from evil is understanding" (Job 28:28).

Abaddon and Death say, "With our ears we have heard a report of it" (Job 28:22).

"The fear of the Lord" and "to depart from evil" are two more virtues that Abaddon and Death do not have, for if they did, it would have been more than just "hearing a report of it;" it would have been in their hearts and kept them from the judgment that awaits them.

During the tribulation, many demonic residents will be released from their Sheol-Hades prison.

One of these is the demon prince who inhabits the Antichrist during part of the tribulation (Rev. 11:7).

Others include the scorpion-centaurs and four wicked angels who will lead the armies of the East into the battle of Armageddon (Rev. 9:13-16).

All of these beings, now confined in Sheol-Hades, are released by God's command.

The four demon angels come out of the nether world from the river Euphrates, which before the great battle will miraculously be dried up (Rev. 16:12). As we noted in chapter 6 (see map of upper Indian Ocean), there is a deep hole at the mouth of the Euphrates in the Persian Sea. This, we said, could be another entrance to Sheol-Hades and coincides with Ivan Sanderson's twelve vortices or holes into the Earth (see chapter 4).

The Infernal Horsemen

The description of this military force on horseback is symbolic. John wrote this in symbolic terminology using the styles of his day to depict these military vehicles and men that will march on Jerusalem.

John saw in this vision two hundred million horsemen

marching from the East over the dried-up Euphrates River. Describing these horsemen in the style of his day, he says:

1. The riders had breastplates of fire, hyacinth and brimstone, similar to the highly reflective mirror-like breastplates of the Roman Legions of John's day.
2. The horses had heads like lions and tails like serpents.
3. Out of the mouths of these horses went fire and smoke that killed one third of mankind—with today's population, approximately 1.3 billion people!
4. The power of these horses was in their heads and tails.
5. Their serpent tails also had heads (Rev. 9:17-19).

Whether this is atomic warfare with some form of military craft is open for conjecture. This, remember, was a vision John saw and he could only put it in the language of his day. He had never seen the military craft of our day.

While the description of this army is open for speculation, we know that this is a modern force led by the four demon angels. We assume, therefore, the two hundred million horsemen are demonized.

It would seem that God is going to allow Satan to have all of his troops back for the major confrontation of the ages in the battle of Armageddon. By this the Lord is saying to all of His creation, "The Lord is greater than all the gods" (Exod. 18:11).

Chapter 9

Creatures of the Deep

*The wicked shall be turned
into hell [Sheol], and all the
nations that forget God
(Psa. 9:17 KJV).*

*In hell [Hades] he lifted up
his eyes, being in torment
. . . And he cried and said
. . . I am tormented in this
flame (Luke 16:23, 24 KJV).*

How many times have you heard the words, "I don't
believe a God of love would allow anyone to go to hell?"

On the surface this is a reasonable question. But we
must deal with another one first:

"Do you believe there is a hell in the world today?"

Most of us would say yes, which leads us to the conclusion:

God, who is living *now*, is allowing a hell to exist in the
present.

If the God of love is allowing a hell to exist today, why
wouldn't He extend it into eternity?

143

In the book *The Revolt of Treblinka,* Jean Francois Steiner tells of the dehumanizing plight of 700,000 Jews—men, women and children—who were exterminated in Treblinka, Poland.

They were gathered from all over Europe and herded like cattle into trains, then transported to Treblinka to be killed. After they had been undressed, they were taken to a room for what they thought was a shower. The shower room instead was quickly filled with poison gas.

Thirteen of these gas chambers were used in 1942 and 1943 in which a total of 2,600 people could be killed every half hour.

Steiner's words of the day before the Jews' mass revolt are descriptive of the abysses of hell:

> The last day of Treblinka: the apocalypse of hell, the end of the nightmare, the world of madness and death was going down amid a lunatic display of fireworks. Its death was true to its life: unreal, distorted, monstrous.

The earthly existence of such hells is a matter of record as six million Jews suffered the same fate.

Or take the infamous Black Dahlia murder of the late 1940s, when a sadist severed a young woman and discarded parts of her mutilated body in a sack in Los Angeles.

Or the numerous beastly killings that happen across the United States each year.

Is there a hell? Does the God of love exist? Where is He? Will He allow anyone to go to hell?

The answer is in Christ, God's Son who died upon the cross.

The God of love looked away from the sin sacrifice, for there hung Christ, representing the ugliness of all humanity. By His death God said to all men, "Sin is ugly; it means

144

death." Sin brings eternal separation from the God of love unless we are willing to accept Christ's sacrifice in payment for our sins.

Jesus Christ on the cross is God reaching out with a heart of love to all who will accept His Word.

What Is Death?

God's Word declares man is a three-part being who is body, soul and spirit. The body is mortal, but the soul and spirit are eternal.

When God breathed into Adam, he became a living being. God formed him out of the earth, like a sculptor would form a statue. After God molded Adam in His image, He gave him part of Himself—an eternal spiritual entity (I Thess. 5:13; Gen. 2:7).

It is this part of man that is eternal; when someone dies, it is the body that returns to dust (Gen. 3:19).

Death means separation; physical death is the separation of the soul and spirit from the body. Spiritual death is the separation of soul and spirit from God.

This separation is the greatest torture awaiting those who reject Christ and die in their sins. There is no way we can grasp the agony of such separation, except from the accounts—both biblical and extrabiblical—of those who have experienced it.

Does God send people to hell? No. But those who reject Christ are drawn there by the power of evil attraction because they have not been transformed by the redemptive power of God in Christ.

Residents of the Deep

We have said that the sea is a cover for a vast underworld civilization that is as old as man himself. It consists of the departed spirits of the human race and of fallen angels from Adam to the present.

God's Word is clear on this. "The wicked shall be turned

into hell [Sheol], and all the nations that forget God," the psalmist wrote.[1]

Job called Sheol the "realm of the dead." [2] It is there that the angels who sinned were committed to "pits of darkness" until the judgment.[3] And it is the place where demons fear to go before their time.[4]

God's Word calls Sheol-Hades a prison for the souls of the ungodly.[5] And it is this underworld region that Jesus described in the story of the rich man and Lazarus.

The rich man was ungodly, and when he died, Jesus said, "in hell [Hades] he lifted up his eyes, being in torments. . . . And he cried and said, Father Abraham, have mercy on me, and send Lazarus, that he may dip the tip of his finger in water, and cool my tongue; for I am tormented in this flame" (Luke 16:23, 24, KJV).

We can learn several things from this story. First, the dead are conscious in Sheol-Hades and second, the dead retain their personalities. In Hades, the rich man could see. He could hear, talk, taste and feel. He had his memory and experienced remorse.

Sheol-Hades is a place of torment. We can only imagine the rich man's shock and despair as he entered the nether world, but it is apparent he was in a place of intense suffering, for he said, "I am tormented in this flame." And there is no escape from this underworld prison (verse 26).

The Bible doesn't give a detailed description of Sheol-Hades. But there have been some in modern times who have traveled in spirit to the nether regions and returned to describe its horrors.

We have gleaned some of these accounts from various sources and condensed them.

While they cannot be placed on the same level as the Scriptures, they give some horrifying glimpses into the identity and fate of the lost. The nature of what they saw—

whether by vision or out of their body in the spirit—is corroborated by Scripture and similar in each account.

When Spirit Leaves Body

Before we consider these accounts, however, let's examine what happens when the spirit leaves the body.

First, it doesn't cease to exist; it goes somewhere.

Wernher von Braun, the famous scientist, says, "I believe in an immortal soul. Science has proved that nothing disintegrates into nothingness. Life and soul, therefore, cannot disintegrate into nothingness, and so are immortal."

Science has no instrument to measure spirit, and so has never been able to follow the flight of the spirit after it leaves the body.

We must turn to God's Word for insight into the spirit, for its principal concern is with the spirit and its eternal destiny. And we can glean knowledge from the testimonies of those who have died, gone to the world beyond and returned to describe it.

We conclude that such experiences can and do occur because there are several occasions in Scripture where mortal man has traveled to or seen into the world beyond, one of which is recorded in II Cor. 12:2-4.

The spirit, after it has left the body, has a definite human form. We seem so bound to concepts of the material world that we tend to disbelieve anything has form and substance in the spirit world. Because something is spirit, this doesn't make it invisible or intangible. Invisibility is relative. The spirit realm about us is invisible only because our eyes aren't adjusted to the spiritual plane.

Not only is there biblical evidence that the spirit has a tangible form, but those who have visited the world beyond say they have seen and talked with departed spirits. And all have touchable form. This is true in both the realms of the lost and of the righteous.

How we can visit the world beyond and come back to tell about it is a mystery known only to God. Some have died and returned through resurrection in answer to prayer. Others, like the Apostle Paul, have been lifted out of their bodies—still alive on Earth—and have been transported in spirit to Heaven or Hades.

One who has visited the regions beyond and returned is George Godkin, a contractor in Alberta, Canada. He gives some interesting insights into the spirit world from his experience recorded in *Voices From the Edge of Eternity.*

When he got over the shock of being out of his body, he became amazed at the vast differences between the physical and spiritual worlds.

First, he says, there is a clear separation of light and darkness.

Second, there is no time factor in the spiritual world.

Third, there is no sense of distance or space.

Fourth, there is a sense of weightlessness when the soul leaves the body.

Fifth, there is a system of order in the resurrected world.

Sixth, there are two distinct places of abode with a great gulf of separation between them.

"There is a Power there that prohibits the individual soul from traveling from one place to another. I stood amazed when I noticed that all classes of people are going to both places.

"Some entered the place of marvelous peace and contentment, while others went into utter darkness, where the agony is something that has never been experienced here on Earth."

He says he wondered why the stream of humanity divides after death—some going to a place of safety and rest and others to a place of agony.

"After I returned to this earthly body, the Spirit of God led me to the Bible, which showed me Christ is the only entrance into the area of eternal pleasure after the death of your mortal body," he says.[6]

As for the wicked dead—those who in this life have rejected Christ—*their spirits yield to the downward pull of Hades. Their spirits are controlled by the law of evil attraction; they become the victims of the prevailing law of the nether world.*

Once in Sheol-Hades, the wicked dead endure suffering for eternity.

We must say here that God never intended for mankind to suffer in Sheol-Hades. It was created for the devil and his angels who rebelled against God. But when mankind rejected God and entered into the sins of Satan, man then became subject to the fate of Satan.

God so loved the world (John 3:16), that He sent Jesus to live as a perfect man so that by His life, death and resurrection He could redeem mankind. And as many as receive Him "to them gave He power to become the sons of God" (John 1:12) and escape the eternal torments of the lost.

Life in the Nether World

Another who has visited the world beyond, Lorne Fox, was permitted to see parts of Heaven and Sheol-Hades. We related much of his story in chapter 5, ending with the part where, under angelic escort, he was taken to a realm where he saw countless lost souls engaged in a variety of tormenting activities.

We now return to his description of this nether world life:

"Not only are the souls of the lost tormented day and night by the fires of hell; but they are tormented, too, by the sins and iniquities which took them there, the things which kept them from acknowledging Christ as Lord and Saviour.

"Hell is *divided!*

"I saw the greatest dancing party ever witnessed. On and on it went with never a stop! Drawing closer, I witnessed features that were convulsed, contorted, twisted with terror and weariness. How they longed to stop . . . but still it continued. Something invisible, sinister, dragged them on in an eternal dance, which they could never stop. I do not hesitate to add that the modern dance hall is one of the devil's biggest trap doors to hell!

"In another place, gambling held sway. Every device, I am sure that has ever been used on Earth . . . and some that have not, are to be found in hell. Vast mountains of gold and silver, gems . . . money. I saw the grasping hands of the greedy, and those that had lusted for money, while on Earth. They reached out to grasp these elusive riches, only to be stung, burned fiercely as they touched them. They would recoil with oaths and curses, and then, as though impelled by some unseen force, they would try and try again . . . and again. . . . That is the horror of hell. The awful repetition . . . the endlessness of it all!

"I saw the proud there! The multitudes who on Earth had been too proud to serve the Lord. Eternally, it seemed, they preened their pride, but loathed it, but the same compelling force demanded that they go on . . . and on. . . .

"I saw a profession of religion there. No worship of God, rather, the worship of self, and of false spirits. The angel of the Lord pointed out these were the people who, on Earth, had completely denied the power of the living Gospel of Christ so the worship of self . . . and of evil spirits . . . went on . . . and on.

"I heard the music of hell! It was a thousand-fold more terrifying than a funeral dirge. It ate into the marrow of the bones.

"I saw fear in hell such as I have never witnessed on

Earth. I have seen tragedy strike during the years of my ministry on Earth. I have seen faces blanched with terror. But I saw this thing magnified one thousand fold in the corridors of hell. I heard anguished cries of fear! I saw the terrorized souls of the lost trying, desperately, to lose themselves in the shadows . . . but to no avail. They were always running from some enemy that did not pursue. . . . The angel said these multitudes were the people who, on Earth, had been too fearful to acknowledge Christ as their Saviour and Lord! Now, in the region of the doomed, their fears, magnified one thousand fold, came back constantly to mock them, to torture them . . . stretching the cords of their emotions on a shuddering rack from which there was no escape!

"Many were the scenes which these mortal eyes beheld, until I felt as though I could bear no more. Always, the comforting presence of the Lord's angel was a mountain of strength to me, or I am certain that I, too, would have been terror stricken!

"I wish I had the power of speech or adequate vocabulary to depict these scenes to you. To sum it up, hell is a thousand times more horrible than words could ever portray in human language!

"God knows the horror of hell. That is why, in His matchless love, He gave His Son to save us from the pit of damnation. How shall you escape the damnation of hell, as the Bible says, except it be through the mercy, love and cleansing blood of Jesus Christ, the eternal Son of God? *I have seen hell!* I entreat you not to ridicule, laugh, scoff! Redemption is yours through Christ, if in humility you will accept Him in your heart." [7]

After this experience, Fox was escorted by the angel into Heaven, where he saw the splendor of God's perfect creation and Holy City—the abode of the righteous dead.

Marietta Davis, a young woman who lived in the mid-1880s, also tells of the horrors she saw in the underworld. We have related a part of her story in chapter 5.

The first place she visited was a world of illusion. As she entered this realm, she could see in the distance what appeared to be vegetation.

"Luminous appearances, like waving trees, with resplendent foliage, and flowers and fruits of crystal and of gold were visible in every direction," she said.

"As I advanced, I walked as upon scorpions, and trod as amid living embers. The trees that seemed to wave about me were fiery exhalations, and their blossoms the sparklings and the burnings of unremitting flames. Each object I approached by contact created agony."

Our interest at this point is her description of the spirits of the lost. She saw multitudes of spirits under the trees. "Some wore crowns upon their heads," she said; "others tiaras; and others decorations of which I knew not the name but which appeared to be wrought of clusters of jewels, wreaths of golden coins, and cloth of gold and silver tissue.

"Others wore towering helmets; and others circlets filled with glistening and waving plumes. A pale phosphorescence was emitted by every object, and all appeared a splendid masquerade.

"The apparel worn by these busy myriads corresponded with the ornaments of the head; hence every variety of sumptuous apparel was displayed upon their forms.

"Kings and queens appeared arrayed in the gorgeous robes of coronation. Groups of nobility of both sexes also were decorated with all the varieties of adornment displayed in the pageantry of kingly courts.

"Dense multitudes were visible in costume proper to the highly cultivated nations; and as they passed by, I discovered similar groups composed of less civilized tribes, attired in barbaric ornaments of every form. While some appeared clothed in the habiliments of the present day, others were in ancient attire; but every class of spirits manifested, in the midst of variety of mode, a uniformity of external pride, pomp and rapidly moving and dazzling lustre."

Could this be one of the scenes and realms witnessed by Fox?

She continues to describe what she heard: "Bursts of laughter—utterances of revelry, of witty ridicule, and polished sarcasm, and obscene allusions and terrible curses broke upon my ear. These again were intermixed with impure solicitations and backbitings, and hollow compliments, and feigned congratulations, and all in one sparkling billiancy, agitated the pained, bewildered sense." [8]

As she experienced the sights and sounds of this horrible realm, the spirit of one she had known on Earth approached. She describes how the spirit looked:

"This being appeared externally far more brilliant than when in the body. The form, the countenance, the eyes, the hands, appeared endued with a metallic lustre that varied with every motion and every thought."

The following is an excerpt from what the spirit told Marietta:

My life on Earth was suddenly brought to a close; and as I departed from the world, *I moved rapidly* in the direction prompted by ruling desires.

I inwardly desired to . . . be free to follow the perverted inclinations of my proud, rebellious and pleasure-loving heart. . . .

With these desires I entered the spirit world, and . . . rushed in haste to the enjoyment of the glittering scenes which you now behold.

I found myself endued with the power of strange and restless motion. I became conscious of a strange pervasion of the brain, and the cerebral organs became subject to a foreign power, which seemed to operate by an absolute possession.

I abandoned myself to the attractive influences that were around me, and sought to satisfy my craving desires for pleasure. I reveled, I banqueted, I mingled in the wild and voluptuous dance, I plucked the shining fruit, I plunged in the ardent streams, I surfeited my nature with that which externally appeared delicious and inviting to the sight and the sense.

But when tasted, all was loathing and the source of increasing pain. And so unnatural are the desires perpetuated here that what I crave I loathe, and that which delights, tortures me.

My tortures create within me a strange intoxication. My appetite is palled, and yet my hunger is unappeased and unappeasable.

Every object which I perceive, I crave, and I grasp it in the midst of disappointment and gather it with increased agony.

I laugh, philosophize, jeer, blaspheme and ridicule by turns. . . .

I inwardly crave to satisfy my hunger and my thirst, and the desire appears to create without and around me a tantalizing illusion of cool waters I may never drink, and grateful fruits I may never taste, and refreshing airs I never feel, and peaceful slumbers I may never enjoy.

I know the forms around me are fantastic and delusive, yet every object appears to hold controlling power, and to domineer with cruel enchantment over my bewildered mind.

I experience the power of the *law of evil attraction*. I am a slave of discordant and deceptive elements. . . .

This realm, curtained with a cloud of nether light, is one sea of perverted and diseased magnetic elements. Here lust, pride, hate, avarice, love of self, ambition, contention and blasphemies, reveling in madness, kindle into a burning flame.

And that specialty of evil which does not belong to and unfold from one spirit, belongs to and unfolds from another; so that the combined strength of the aggregate of all, is the prevailing law. By this strength of evil I am bound, and in it I exist.

Here also sense is infinitely more acute . . . in like proportion is the consciousness and capability of suffering here, superior to human suffering.[9]

The lost spirit didn't blame God for its fate. "We were advised of the consequences of our course while in the body," it said. "But we loved our ways better than those which exalted the soul. We have fallen into this fearful abode. We have originated our sorrow. *God is just. He is good. We know that 'tis not from a vindictive law of our Creator that we suffer.*

"Marietta," the spirit continued, "it is our condition from which we receive the misery we endure. The violation of the moral law, by which our moral natures should have been preserved in harmony and health, is the prime cause of our state.

155

"O sin!" the spirit lamented. "Thou parent of countless woes! Thou insidious enemy of peace and Heaven! Why do mortals love thy ways?"

Marietta said she was filled with terror as she listened to the spirit and felt its eyes, wild with despair, upon her. She tried to escape, but the spirit cried out, "No, Marietta, leave me not; can you not endure for a short period the sight and relation of what I am continually suffering? Tarry with me, for I desire to speak many things."

Realm of Hopelessness

The spirit described its realm as a land of hopelessness; a realm filled with the haunting memories of lost opportunities where evil forms the external sphere of a lost soul's existence.

On Earth, the spirit said, evil is invisible and interior. But in the nether world, it is "our outward dwelling." It is a realm where souls, remembering the days of love and mortal peace, are filled with the madness and delirium of remorse. And adding to this torment is the pain of recognition. Spirits who had known each other while mortal beings on Earth, recognize each other in hell.

Marietta was overcome by this and was immediately removed from this realm.

Marietta said she passed into a sphere where the darkness was more dense, and the condition of its resident spirits was "more desperate than those from whom I had just escaped."

Here she witnessed the utter despair of the religious hypocrites and the bitter incriminations of those who followed false religious leaders. The knowledge of God's Word and the bitter memories of their rejection of it were part of their torture. Here the spirits seemed agitated.

At the end of her visit, an angel of the Lord explained the sights as the consequences of sin upon the spirit of man.

"Spiritual sufferings are beyond any power of expression," the angel explained.

"Marietta, thy spirit cannot endure more; but let this lesson impress thee with the great truth, that 'the wages of sin is death.' " [10]

Lake of Molten Fire

Others who have seen into the regions of the lost say they have seen a lake of molten fire "in a semi-dark pit from which arose clouds of smoke. When the smoke settled low, the fire in the lake was less distinct. When the smoke lifted a little, the burning lake with red and greenish flames and its inmates could be distinctly seen.

"The lost were seen going into hell. Some fell in, some walked over the brink, and some were bound by demon chains and cast into hell by demons.

"When the fire abated and the smoke settled down the moans of the miserable could be heard. When the fire at intervals increased in intensity and the smoke lifted a little, there were shrieks and wails of agony.

"In the lake of fire were oceans of hands reaching up for help." [11]

Evangelist Kenneth Hagen says he was once escorted by the Lord to Sheol-Hades. Here is his account:

> We went down to hell, and as we went into that place I saw what appeared to be human beings wrapped in flames. [12]

In each of these accounts and descriptions there are striking similarities. And there is amazing corroboration of the agonies of Sheol-Hades indicated by God's Word.

Population Explosion

The population of Sheol-Hades is ever increasing. To accommodate its population explosion, the nether world may have to be enlarged periodically—a possibility indicated in Scripture.

The Bible says "Hell [Sheol] has enlarged thyself" (Isa. 5:14). Here Isaiah is speaking about the death of Israel during the Babylonian invasion.

About 60 million people lost their lives during World War II. Many of the disappearances in the Bermuda Triangle happened during and after such major wars. Is there a connection? Are the physical disturbances in the Triangle indications that Sheol-Hades is again enlarging itself? We can only speculate of course. But it is interesting to note that Sheol enlarged itself during the Babylonian invasion, and far greater numbers have died in modern wars.

Mankind need not go there. God in love respects the free moral agency of man. He will accommodate man by letting him have what he wants, though every man has an alternative. And the alternative is this: the Christ of Calvary died for sinners, giving His life in atonement for sin.

Christ's death was substitutionary. He took our judgment, our penalty for our transgressions. These words, "sin and death came by Moses but life and grace came by Jesus Christ," show the contrasts between sin and grace, life and death.

Grace is weakened without sin, for what free gift is there without indebtedness? What joy is there when one receives what he deserves?

What freedom is there to one who has never been bound? Or what triumph is there to one who has never been victorious? And what restful peace is there to one who has never been at war?

What relief is there to the one who has never been in pain?

In our day the cross has been weakened by cheap grace

and bargain-basement prices; it costs us nothing. It has been watered down with lack of sacrifice, lack of dedication, and lack of self denial.

Heaven did cost something; it cost God the life of His Son in atonement for our sins.

If there is no Heaven to lose, then Christ died in vain. But if Christ's sacrifice was to forgive us our debt of sin, and His resurrection was to give us a new life—what victory, what relief, what joy!

If there is no eternal retribution and judgment and no separation of the corrupt and their corruption from Heaven, then we would not want to go there.

We cannot lose sight of the great cost of the cross. It is the total sacrifice for another—for you and me. Those who have found this love can rejoice in its deliverance and find peace in death.

But those who reject this love and sacrifice must pay their own penalty for sin—in the nether world abode of the wicked dead.

Chapter 10

The End
of the World

*And I saw a new heaven
and a new earth; for the
first heaven and the first
earth passed away, and
there is no longer any sea
(Rev. 21:1).*

How long will the wicked dead stay in the nether realms? When will they be judged, and what will happen to them after the judgment?

Will the lost be sealed forever in a fiery tomb beneath the sea—forgotten by God and the hosts of Heaven?

What are God's plans for the nether realms once He has established His eternal kingdom on Earth? Will He permit a place of torment to coexist with a world restored to its original perfection and crowned with the glories of His eternal throne?

And what about the sea? It is the receptacle of man's pollutions and wastes; it is a cover for a vast underworld civilization of departed spirits. Will it continue to hide the hideousness of man's past throughout the ages of eternity? Or will the mysteries of the sea be uncovered so all may look into the regions of the damned?

We have shown in the opening chapters of this book that the sea has been the key to man's past.

Evolutionists say life originated in the sea. Occultists trace their origins to lost continents beneath it. And geologists have searched under the sea to find clues to the age and composition of our planet.

We have examined the mysteries of the Bermuda Triangle and the strange disappearances and phenomena reported by mariners, pilots and other witnesses of the unusual and bizarre. We have observed the natural phenomena of the Triangle and examined the causes behind physical disturbances and theories in the area.

We have traced the history and theories of Triangle legends and have noted their ties with the occult. We also have noted the presence of UFOs in the Triangle and explained the spiritual significance of their strange capabilities and purposes.

And we have discussed the existence of a parallel world, a dimension inhabited by spirits—good and evil.

We have said that while a great percentage of the disappearances and other phenomena of the Triangle can be attributed to natural causes, there is enough of the mysterious and unexplainable to arouse questions that must be answered. And our thesis has been that whether explainable or not, entities from the parallel world are involved in the physical world.

We have said that diabolical entities are behind much of the physical disturbances in the Triangle, and we have laid the biblical foundation for this conclusion.

We noted that spirit entities are not bound by time and

The *Sylvia L. Ossa,* shown here docked in New Orleans in March, 1975, disappeared with its thirty-seven crewmen in the Bermuda Triangle in mid-October, 1976. It was a Panamanian cargo ship and measured 590 feet in length.

can provide knowledge about the ancient past as well as the future, but we have taken such revelations seriously only where they can be supported by Scripture.

The theories of such cultists as Edgar Cayce, Darwin Gross, Ed Snedeker, M.B. Dykshoorn and others have been examined and compared to biblical truth.

We have shown positive evidence that the entities of the parallel world are intruding into the material realm in pursuit of a diabolical plan to drag today's world toward disaster—just as they did just before the great Noahic Flood.

And we have noted the effects of these entities on the hearts and minds of humanity, that the theories they create—while bordering on the ridiculous—are riddled with fantasies, containing elements of truth that cannot be ignored.

163

In all of these, we see biblical prophecies concerning the coming of God's kingdom being fulfilled. The reality of this fact, we have said, puts fear into the hearts of fallen angelic beings and the disembodied spirits who once lived on Earth under Lucifer's reign before he rebelled against God.

We have noted how these evil entities take refuge in the dreams of their former home, while Satan propagates false religions to support this fantasy.

Satan today is glamorizing his hereditary birthplace by psychics, who trace their origins to a former continent and a lost civilization that some claim still exist in the nether part of the Earth.

And occultists are saying there are entrances to the nether world at various points around the globe, including one in the depths of the Bermuda Triangle.

We have contrasted these theories with the reality of truth. There *is* a nether world, and its entrances are in the sea. Could these entrances be in the area theorized by the psychics? We can only speculate. But we do know this: the nether world is the abode of departed spirits awaiting judgment by God.

Satan is paranoid with the fantasy that these departed spirits are still part of his kingdom. God is capable of defeating the enemy at full force, but Satan still thinks he can whip God.

And as the world draws nearer to the climactic confrontation between Satan and God, we are experiencing intense and evil intrusions from the spirit realm into the physical world.

For thousands of years, the Bermuda Triangle has been clouded with legends. Much of the mystery has been fabricated, sometimes for the sheer pleasure of sensationalism. But even in the explainable, even in the natural, the element of mystery can be found in that much of what occurs in the Triangle has other-world significance.

We have shown from the Scriptures *who* is behind both the mysterious and the explainable and why. Even in the fabricated mysteries of the sea, we can see the hand and purpose of the real perpetrators of intrigue—to bring glamor to Lucifer's former kingdom, part of which is now beneath the sea.

The mystery has been solved. God's Word lifts the shroud.

We can see from Scripture how God uses the natural and physical elements for deliverance, spiritual lessons and judgment. And we see how Satan uses them for destruction and deception.

A host of spirit beings—good and evil—whose acts—whether godly or diabolical—are affecting the lives of every person on this planet.

Yes, the mystery is solved, but the drama continues.

One scene in this continuing drama is the pollution of the seas. In the second bowl judgment of the final seven bowls of wrath is the death of life in the seas. The Bible says:

> And the second angel poured out his bowl into the
> sea* and it became blood like that of a dead man;
> and every living thing in the sea died (Rev. 16:3).

We are living close to this prediction with today's pollution of the seas. If present conditions continue, scientists say our seas could reach a point of no return in pollution within the next few years.

Take Howard Gruft's findings of the mycobacterial infections, for example. He says the infections are coming from the Atlantic Ocean along the seacoast from Virginia to

---

* Some commentators say this is only the Mediterranean Sea.

Florida. Gruft is from the New York State Department of Health in Albany, New York. He presented these findings to the American Lung Association in New Orleans at one of their recent meetings. He said mycobacteria can survive in ocean waters for long periods of time. He found that these organisms in ocean water can be released into the air through (rain) droplets . . . and are small enough to penetrate the tiniest airways of the lung.[1]

Also, concerning pollution, Jacques Cousteau says, "the Mediterranean Sea is so sick that only a carefully coordinated program on a massive scale can avert the disaster." [2]

With the prophecy of Rev. 16:3 stating that every living thing in the sea will die, we can now see the events leading up to the fulfillment of that prophecy. When the seas finally reach total pollution, will their purpose come to an end?

The Bible says no. God has a purification plant that will be turned on after the return of Christ and will continue to purify the oceans for one thousand years. Only then will the purpose of the seas come to their final destiny, for in the new heavens and the new Earth there will be "no more sea" (Rev. 21:1).

Waters and Earth Purified

Following the second coming of Christ, after the battle of Armageddon, there will be a gigantic cleanup operation.

Israel will use discarded military equipment for fuel for seven years to heat homes (Ezek. 39:9-10).

It will take seven months to bury the dead bodies of the slain armies (Ezek. 39:11-16).

And God will put an ocean purification system under the temple in Jerusalem to cleanse the polluted seas. These living waters will be divided so that half will flow to the Mediterranean and half out to the Dead Sea (Zech. 14:8).

The Bible says:

Then said he unto me, These waters issue out to-

ward the east country, and go down into the desert,
and go into the sea: which being brought forth into
the sea, the waters shall be healed. And it shall
come to pass that every thing that liveth, which
moveth, whithersoever the river shall come, shall
live: and there shall be a very great multitude of
fish, because these waters shall come thither: for
they shall be healed; and every thing shall live
whither the river cometh (Ezek. 47:8-9 KJV).

This miracle river will not only cleanse the seas but
restore life; its banks will flourish with fruit orchards and the
leaves of trees lining the banks will be used for medicine
(Ezek. 47:12).

Thus God will restore the seas for their continued use
for another thousand years. During this period Sheol-Hades
will continue to hold all the unrighteous since the time of
Adam, and the devil will be "bound" in it for a thousand
years (Rev. 20:1-2).

The Earth then will be free of the influence of evil for a
thousand years, Christ will rule from Jerusalem with his
saints and this world will again be reinhabited for its final
hour.

By this the Lord is saying to all generations that man
can live in peace free from pollution if they allow the Prince
of Peace to have control.

At the end of this millennium, Satan will be released
from his prison. This final test of allegiance will only be for
the people and their offspring who survived the tribulation
period. Because death will no longer reign, the world will
reach its greatest population.[3]

It is hard to believe that the number of people who will
follow Satan after living under the rule of Christ for a
thousand years "is like the sand of the seashore" (Rev. 20:8).

However, one only has to be reminded of the children of Israel *after* their miraculous deliverance out of Egypt when they rebelled and made the golden calf, for one to understand the total depravity of human nature (Exod. 32:7-10).

This final battle will involve "Gog and Magog" (Rev. 20:8). Fire will come down from Heaven and devour the hosts of Gog and Magog as they surround Jerusalem (Rev. 20:9).

After this, the nether regions will be emptied. Satan's counterfeits will be exposed, and mankind will see the fulfillment of God's eternal purposes for Earth.

God's Word says there's a new world coming in which His perfect Earth will be restored.

> And I saw a new heaven and new earth; for the first
> heaven and the first earth passed away, and there
> is no longer any sea (Rev. 21:1).

The day is coming when the sea will give up its dead. Death and Hades will give up their dead. And all the wicked now existing in the nether regions will be brought before the great judgment.

The books will be opened and sentences pronounced. Death and Hades and all its residents will be cast into Gehenna, a "lake of fire" (Rev. 20:11-15). Satan also will be cast into this lake "and shall be tormented day and night for ever and ever" (verse 10).

Thus ends the Sheol-Hades abode for the departed spirits of lost humanity and fallen angels.

The location of Gehenna (lake of fire) is open for conjecture. But Dr. Finis Dake believes that it will be accessible for all to see, based upon his interpretation of Isa. 66:22-24.[4]

The present world will come to an end with the judgment at the end of the thousand-year reign of Christ. The

Earth will be renovated and remade (II Pet. 2:8-13), and there will be no more sea.

The sea had been God's reservoir for good and bad; it had supplied us with rains and purified our refuse. It had purged the Earth on two occasions by floods and held its captives till the end of time. God's purposes for the sea will come to an end.

Its storms will blow no longer on Earth, for its judgment will have ceased.

There *will* be water on the new Earth, but it will no longer hide the despicable or make havoc with its unharnessed forces. In God's new Earth, it will bring life.

John the revelator saw a pure river of water, clear as crystal, proceeding from the throne of God in the new world. On each side of the river is planted the tree of life. God has always intended water for life, but to a fallen humanity, water became a force for destruction.

The source of this water of life is Jesus Christ. Just as in the kingdom to come all may partake of the water of life freely (Rev. 22:17), so today Jesus says, "If any man thirst, let him come unto me, and drink. He that believeth on me, as the Scripture hath said, out of his belly shall flow rivers of living water" (John 7:37, 38).

God's Word says:

> . . . "Come." And let the one who hears say, "Come." And let the one who is thirsty come; let the one who wishes take the water of life without cost (Rev. 22:17).

APPENDIXES

I

(for chapter one)

Spirit Beings Behind UFO Phenomenon

Some of the most intelligent people in the world believe in UFOs.

A recent survey showed that 93 per cent of the 322-member French branch of Mensa International, the exclusive organization of people with exceptionally high IQs, believe UFOs are real.*

And a 1973 Gallup Poll indicated that 15 million adult Americans have personally seen one.

In recent years, however, the number of UFO sightings has dramatically increased. Statistics show 10,000 recorded sightings before 1954; since then, sightings in the millions have been reported around the world.

But while millions have seen and believe in UFOs, there is considerable disagreement over the nature of the craft and who is behind the phenomenon.

UFO Theories

A number of theories exist, which try to explain the presence and nature of UFOs. Theories say UFOs are:

1. Physical craft from another world.
2. Semi-solid or semi-physical craft from another dimension.

---

* *National Enquirer*, June 10, 1975.

3. Creatures, not machines. Craft we see may be outer shells of the creatures.
4. Spectral, ghostlike; luminous, but nonmaterial.
5. An enemy weapon.
6. Craft created or operated by demons.

John Weldon in *UFOs: What On Earth Is Happening?* examines these theories and concludes that UFOs are demonic:

> Today the sightings [of UFOs] are accelerating in number, with the last thirty years presenting a virtual explosion of this phenomenon. Something definitely is up.

> We think demons are behind this startling phenomenon, and we think their activity is connected with the upcoming Tribulation period. Viewed in this context, the activity of demons at this particular time is not at all surprising or strange.

Link with Occult

There is an obvious link between UFOs and the occult. An examination of Scripture will show similarities between the activities of demons and what is being experienced with UFOs.

Demon *possession*, the indwelling of human beings, occurs in some UFO contactee cases. In the Bible, demons are said to seek rest in human bodies (Luke 8:30; 11:24-26; Matt. 12:43-45) and animals (Matt. 8:30-32).

The Bible also says demons can *imitate good spirits* (II Cor. 11:14, 15) and *predict the future* (Acts 16:16); they also can *manipulate the human mind* (John 13:2; Matt. 13:19, 39) and *project false realities* (Matt. 4:8).

Weldon says:

> Contactees almost uniformly report (at least initially) the benevolence of their UFO contacts, and they often receive predictions of the future which later, in many cases, prove to be false. They also report the extraterrestrials' ability to exert full control over their minds and perceptions.

Angels are capable of assuming human form (Gen. 19:1-11; Luke 1:26; John 20:12; Acts 12:19) and make contact with human beings (Gen. 1:10; Heb. 13:2). They can materialize and dematerialize at will (Luke 2:9, 13, 15), and they have great power (Psa. 103:20; II Thess. 1:7; II Pet. 2:11) and can kill (II Sam. 24:17; II Kings 19:35; I Chron. 21:12-16; Acts 12:23).

In connection with the capabilities of angels, Weldon says:

> Demons, we should remember, are the same as good angels, only fallen. As such, they would have similar power to the pure angels but would use them for evil instead of good (Dan. 10:12, 13).

It is interesting to note that most of the powers and abilities of biblical angels (most of them fallen) can be applied to the powers of UFOs or their occupants. It is not strange, then, that people say they have seen UFO beings. We believe the beings are none other than evil entities in tangible form.

Weldon says UFOs and their accompanying occult phenomena are manifestations of the final battles between the spirits in the parallel world. Demons and fallen angels have something special against God. And the Bible indicates that the forces of good and evil are in combat in the invisible world. Indeed, we are involved in this warfare as Paul says in Eph. 6:12:

> We are not fighting against people made of flesh and blood, but against persons without bodies—the evil rulers of the unseen world, those mighty satanic beings and great evil princes of darkness who rule this world; and against huge numbers of wicked spirits in the spirit world (Living Bible).

UFOs and their occupants represent overt demon activity in the material world. The theory that UFOs are physical craft from another world is widely accepted. And this serves a useful purpose to the parallel world. Weldon has some interesting speculation at this point:

> In our demon theory contact is not only possible but certainly expected. The operators of the UFOs, as we see it, have come expressly to contact human beings.

> The most frightening possibility of all, from the point of view of biblical prophecy, is that somebody will step out of a UFO with solutions to our world problems. A leading social psychologist feels that many people would actually welcome a humanoid being from another planet and might even set him up as a messiah or religious leader. This superior alien, with technological knowledge beyond our grasp, could effect what we might regard as miracles.

Further evidence of demon influence behind UFOs is seen in the fact that many people interested in them are involved in various occult societies and spiritualism.

Lynn E. Catoe, a bibliographer who compiled *UFOs and Related Subjects: An Annotated Bibliography*, published by the U.S. Government Printing Office, says:

> A large part of the available UFO literature is closely linked with mysticism and the metaphysical. It deals with subjects like mental telepathy, automatic writing and invisible entities. . . .

> Many of the UFO reports now being published in the popular press recount alleged incidents that are strikingly similar to demoniac possession and psychic phenomena which have long been known to theologians and parapsychologists.

Standard tools of the occult often are used in establishing contact with UFOs, including a ouija board, trance dictation, mentally perceived voices (a common occult phenomenon), levitation, telethought, teleportation (transportation of persons from place to place without physical means) and telekinesis (transportation of material objects).

An even more ominous tie is seen by John A. Keel who correlates the sinister acts of the Illuminati cult and certain UFO phenomena. The Illuminati are associated with witchcraft and black magic and are suspected of manipulating world governments and their economic policies in a drive toward one-world government, which the Bible says will be led by a diabolically possessed man whom it calls Antichrist.

If occultists in the Bible (Exodus 7:9-12, 22; 8:7) can manipulate and transform matter through the power of evil entities, it can readily be seen how modern psychics can show similar powers.

With the power to change matter it is conceivable that spirit entities could take anything material and transform it into a UFO, assume human form, and land openly to prove the existence of visitors from outer space. UFOs also could be demonically induced mental projections or temporary manipulations of matter and energy.

However they manage to do it, spirit entities have millions of believers in UFOs historically and worldwide. And incidents are increasing dramatically. Something is up. As Weldon puts it, "Quite simply, we think the demons are preparing the coming of Antichrist."

Intermarriage of Angels with Mankind

Spirit entities precipitated the Noahic Flood. They are again setting mankind up for destruction. Again the past is a key to the future. Note Gen. 6:1-5:

> Now it came about, when man began to multiply on the face of the land, and daughters were born to them, that the sons of God saw that the daughters of men were beautiful; and they took wives for themselves, whomever they chose.
>
> Then the LORD said, 'My Spirit shall not strive with man forever, because he also is flesh. . . .'
>
> The Nephilim [giants] were on the earth in those days, and also afterward, when the sons of God came in to the daughters of men, and they bore children to them. Those were the mighty men who were of old, men of renown.
>
> Then the LORD saw that the wickedness of man was great on the earth, and that every intent of the thoughts of his heart was only evil continually.

The generally accepted interpretation of this passage is that the "sons" of God were the angels who had rebelled against God. These angels were able to mingle with mankind. It isn't surprising, then, that ancient cultures have recorded the presence of supernatural beings, which usually come from the skies.

The passage also signifies that not all the "sons" of God are good.

Humanity became so wicked that it accepted demons as marriage partners, an act so abominable to God that His only solution was judgment by worldwide catastrophe.

Today there is ready acceptance of supernatural entities just as in the days before the Flood. This gives interesting insight into Jesus' comment:

> For the coming of the Son of Man will be just like the days of Noah (Matt. 24:37).

The Bible indicates that the vast majority of mankind will be demonized shortly before Armageddon. In the process, Earth will suffer massive geological upheavals and global catastrophies not experienced in the history of man.

II

(for chapter two)

Bible Synopsis on Luciferian and Noahic Floods

There were two universal destructions by floods in the ancient past.

The Luciferian Flood was the first, which took place between 11,000 and 9000 B.C., climaxing the ice age.

The Noahic Flood followed between 7000 and 5000 B.C., ending the Antediluvians of Noah's day.

The following are contrasts between the two floods:

LUCIFERIAN	NOAHIC
1. *Earth was formless*	*Dove brought back a fresh olive leaf*
"And the earth was formless" (Gen. 1:2).	". . . dove came to him . . . in her beak was a freshly picked olive leaf" (Gen. 8:11).
The Hebrew word for formless is *tohu* and is in Psa. 107:40 and "city of *confusion*" in Isa. 24:10.	The Lord had not destroyed *all* life, only man and non-marine life. God preserved pairs of all animals and eight persons.
2. *Earth was void*	*Animals kept alive on the Ark.*
"And the earth was void" (Gen. 1:2).	"And of every living thing of all flesh, you shall bring two of every kind into the ark" (Gen. 6:19).

"In the beginning God created the heavens and the earth" (Gen. 1:1).

This verse is a summary statement. The Hebrew idiom gives the summary and then the details. For example:

Hebrew would say, "A man . . . a good one."

English would say, "A good man."

Hence verse one is a summary, and verses 2 to 31 include the details. Gen. 2:1-4 finishes the summary statement of Gen. 1:1.

"In the beginning God created the heavens and the earth" (summary statement).

"Let there be light" (Gen. 1:3).

"God called the expanse Heaven" (Gen. 1:8).

"Let dry land appear" (Gen. 1:9).

"Let the earth sprout vegetation" (Gen. 1:11).

"Let there be lights" (Gen. 1:14).

"Let the waters teem with swarms of living creatures, and let birds fly above the earth . . ." (Gen. 1:20).

"And God created the great sea monsters . . ." (Gen. 1:21).

(These are the details of the summary statement in verses 2-31 of Gen. 1). Then God locks in the details by repeating the summary:

> Thus the heavens and the earth were completed, and all their hosts . . . then God blessed the seventh day . . . because in it He rested from all His work which God had created and made. This is the account of the heavens and the earth when they were created, in the day that the Lord God made earth and heaven (Gen. 2:1-4).

This statement locks in the details of chapter 1. The words "thus" and "this is the account" go with the details of chapter 1.

In verse 2 we have "formless" (Heb. *tohu*) and "void" (Heb. *bohu*). A paraphrase of verse 2 could read:

> Now this was the way things were when God took the Earth and transformed it from chaos into a cosmos.

It was a wilderness, in confusion (through the fall of Lucifer) and was void and lifeless. Verse 1 is a summary statement of the six days, not the original creation though it could include it. There are many Scriptures on the original creation without using Gen. 1:1, i.e., Isa. 45:18, Job 38, Psa. 8:3, 19:1, and Acts 17:24.

In the details of Earth's renovation in days 1-3, God is overcoming *tohu*—chaos. In days 4-6, God is overcoming *bohu*—lifeless.

> I looked on the earth, and behold, it was formless and void;
>
> And to the heavens, and they had no light. I looked on the mountains, and behold, they were quaking,
>
> And all the hills moved to and fro. I looked, and behold, there was no man, And all the birds of the heavens had fled. I looked, and behold, the fruitful land was a wilderness,
>
> And all its cities were pulled down before the LORD, before His fierce anger (Jer. 4:23-26).

Tohu—chaotic, empty	*Renovation—overcoming tohu*
Heavens had no light, (Jer. 4:23).	First day—heavens had light again, (Gen. 1:3-5).
Mountains quaking, hills moved to and fro, (Jer. 4:24).	Second day—dry land appeared and waters gathered into one place and called seas, (Gen. 1:9-10).
Fruitful land was a wilderness, (Jer. 4:26).	Third day—Earth brought forth vegetation, the trees bearing fruit, (Gen. 1:12).
Cities were pulled down (social order destroyed)—*cosmos*, (II Pet. 3:6)—the then world standing out of water.	Cain built a city and called it Enoch—beginning of social order, (Gen. 4:17).

Bohu—lifeless	*Replenishing—overcoming bohu*
No birds, (Jer. 4:25).	Fifth day—" . . . and let the birds fly above the earth in the open expanse of the heavens" (Gen. 1:20).
No man.	Sixth day—"Let Us make man in Our image, according to Our likeness . . ." (Gen. 1:26).

3. *Earth made totally dark*	*Not made totally dark*
". . . and darkness was over the surface of the deep . . ." (Gen. 1:2). ". . . And to the heavens and they had no light" (Jer. 4:23).	". . . And the dove came to him toward evening. . . . waited yet another seven days . . ." (Gen. 8:11-12).

Not only was the Earth left in chaotic condition after the fall of Lucifer, but verse 2 says:

"And darkness was over the surface of the deep. . . ."

This darkness implies something was wrong and evil. Satan is allied with darkness in Scripture, while God is always light.

4. *No light from Heaven*	*Light from Heaven*
". . . and darkness was over the surface of the deep . . ." (Gen. 1:2).	". . . at the end of forty days, that Noah opened the window of the ark which he had made. . . . So he waited yet another seven days; and again he sent out the dove from the ark. And the dove came to him toward evening. . . . Then he waited yet another seven days . . ." (Gen. 8:6, 10, 11, 12).

5. *No days*

"And God saw that the light was good; and God separated the light from the darkness. And God called the light day, and the darkness He called night. And there was evening and there was morning, one day" (Gen. 1:4-5).

Days

". . . end of forty days . . . yet another seven days . . . toward evening . . . yet another seven days. . . . And in the second month, on the twenty-seventh day of the month, the earth was dry" (Gen. 8:6-14).

6. *All vegetation destroyed*

"And the earth was formless and void. . . . Let the earth sprout vegetation, plants yielding seed, and fruit trees bearing fruit after their kind, with seed in them, on the Earth . . ." (Gen. 1:2-11).

". . . And the earth brought forth vegetation, plants yielding seed after their kind, and trees bearing fruit with seed in them, after their kind . . ." (Gen. 1:12).

Vegetation left

"And the dove came to him toward evening; and behold in her beak was a freshly picked olive leaf. . ." (Gen. 8:11).

7. *No continual receding of waters off the Earth*

"Then God said, 'Let there be an expanse in the midst of the waters, and let it separate the waters from the waters'" (Gen. 1:6).

Continual receding of waters off the Earth

"and the water receded steadily from the earth, and at the end of one hundred and fifty days the water decreased. . . . And the water decreased steadily until the tenth month . . . on the first day of the month, the tops of the mountains became visible" (Gen. 8:3-5).

8. *Waters taken off the Earth in one day*

"Then God said, 'Let the waters below the heavens be gathered into one place, and let the dry land appear'; and it was so" (Gen. 1:9).

Took a month for the waters to abate

"Now it came about in the six hundred and first year, in the first *month*, on the first of the month, the water was dried up from the earth. Then Noah removed the covering of the ark, and looked, and behold, the surface of the ground was dried up. And in the second month, on the twenty-seventh day of the month, the earth was dry" (Gen. 8:13-14).

9. *Supernatural working of taking waters off the Earth*

"Then God said, 'Let there be an expanse in the midst of the waters, and let it separate the waters from the waters. . . . Let the waters below the heavens be gathered into one place, and let the dry land appear' " (Gen. 1:6, 9).

Natural work of taking waters off the Earth

"And the water receded steadily from the earth, and at the end of one hundred and fifty days the water decreased. . . . And the water decreased steadily until the tenth month . . ." (Gen. 8:3-5).

10. *God rebuked the waters*

"Thou didst cover it with the deep as with a garment; the waters were standing above the mountains. At Thy rebuke they fled" (Psa. 104:6).

No rebuke of the waters

"But God remembered Noah and all the beasts and all the cattle that were with him in the ark; and God caused a wind to pass over the Earth, and the water subsided" (Gen. 8:1).

11. *Waters hasted away*

". . . At the sound of Thy thunder they hurried away" (Psa. 104:7).

Waters gradually receded

"And the water receded steadily from the earth, and at the end of one hundred and fifty days the water decreased. . . . And the water decreased steadily until the tenth month; in the tenth month . . . the tops of the mountains became visible" (Gen. 8:3-5).

12. *God set a bound for waters*

"Thou didst set a boundary that they may not pass over; That they may not return to cover the earth" (Psa. 104:99).

Bounds already set

"Then God said, 'Let the waters below the heavens be gathered into one place, and let the dry land appear'; and it was so" (Gen. 1:9).

"Also the fountains of the deep and the floodgates of the sky were closed, and the rain from the sky was restrained" (Gen. 8:2).

13. *All fish destroyed*

Because sun withheld from Earth (possible reason why only marine life that is pre-Adamic is found in the ocean depths where there is no light).

". . . darkness over face of deep . . . let the waters teem with swarms of living creatures . . . and God created great sea monsters. . . ." (Gen. 1:2, 20-21).

". . . And to the heavens, and they had no light . . ." (Jer. 4:23).

No fish destroyed—only land animals

"And of every living thing of all flesh, you shall bring two of every kind into the ark to keep them alive with you . . . of birds . . . of the animals . . . of every creeping thing of the ground" (Gen. 6:19-20).

"Every beast, every creeping thing, and every bird, every thing that moves on the earth, went out . . . from the ark" (Gen. 8:19).

185

14. *No fowls*

Fowls preserved

". . . And all the birds of the heavens had fled" (Jer. 4:25).

"And of every living thing of all flesh . . . of the birds after their kind" (Gen. 6:19-20).

". . . and let birds fly above the earth in the open expanse of the heavens" (Gen. 1:20).

"Bring out with you every living thing of all flesh that is with you, birds . . ." (Gen. 8:17).

15. *No animals left*

Animals preserved

"Then God said, 'Let the earth bring forth living creatures after their kind: cattle and creeping things and beast of the earth after their kind' " (Gen. 1:24).

"And of every living thing of all flesh, you shall bring two of every kind into the ark, to keep them alive with you; they shall be male and female" (Gen. 6:19).

"And out of the ground the LORD God formed every beast of the field . . ." (Gen. 2:19).

16. *No man left*

Eight men and women saved

"Then God said, 'Let Us make man in Our image, according to Our likeness; and let them rule over the fish of the sea and over the birds of the sky and over the cattle and over all the earth. . . .'

". . . during the construction of the ark, in which a few, that is, eight persons, were brought safely through the water" (I Pet. 3:20).

"And God created man in His own image . . . male and female He created them" (Gen. 1:26-27).

"I looked, and behold there was no man . . ." (Jer. 4:25).

17. *No social system left*

". . . and the earth was formed out of water and by water, through which the world at that time was destroyed, being flooded with water" (II Pet. 3:5-6).

"I looked, and behold, the fruitful land was a wilderness. And all its cities were pulled down before the LORD, before His fierce anger" (Jer. 4:26).

A social system left

"But I will establish My convenant with you; and you shall enter the ark—you and your sons and your wife, and your sons' wives with you" (Gen. 6:18).

"While the earth remains, seedtime and harvest, and cold and heat, and summer and winter, and day and night shall not cease" (Gen. 8:22).

". . . but preserved Noah, a preacher of righteousness, with seven others, when He brought a flood upon the world of the ungodly;" (II Pet. 2:5).

18. *No ark made to save life*

". . . the world at that time was destroyed, being flooded with water" (II Pet. 3:6).

No ark mentioned.

". . . there was no man . . . and all the cities were pulled down . . ." (Jer. 4:25-26).

An ark made to save life

". . . during the construction of the ark, in which a few, that is, eight persons, were brought safely through the water" (I Pet. 3:20).

19. *Cause: fall of Lucifer*

"How art thou fallen from heaven, O Lucifer, son of the morning! . . . Yet thou shalt be brought down to hell [Sheol], to the sides of the pit" (Isa. 14:12-15 KJV).

(This isn't fulfilled until Rev. 20:3, when Satan is cast into the bottomless pit during the millenial reign of Christ.)

". . . you were the anointed cherub who covers, and I placed you there . . . therefore I have cast you as profane from the mountain of God. And I have *destroyed you, O covering cherub* . . ." (Ezek. 28:14-19).

"And He said to them, 'I was watching Satan fall from heaven like lightning' " (Luke 10:18).

20. *Result: tohu and bohu— formless and void*

It became necessary to make new fish, fowl, land animals, man, vegetation.

Cause: wickedness of man and fallen angels—daughters of men marrying sons of God.

"Now it came about, when men began to multiply on the face of the land and daughters were born to them, that the sons of God saw that the daughters of men were beautiful; and they took wives for themselves, whomever they chose. Then the LORD said, 'My Spirit shall not strive with man forever, because he also is flesh, nevertheless his days shall be one hundred and twenty years.' The Nephilim [giants—offspring of marriage— daughters of men and sons of God], were on the earth in those days . . ." (Gen. 6:1-4).

"And angels who did not keep their own domain, but abandoned their proper abode, He has kept in eternal bonds under darkness . . ." (Jude 6).

Result: no new creation made

All things were preserved, except Antediluvians who are chained in hell (Gr. Tartarus). Another compartment in the nether world— there are compartments in Sheol-Hades—*Paradise* (Abraham's bosom), *hell* (Hades compartment where rich man was—Luke 16:22-23), *Tartarus* (where fallen Nephilim giants are confined).

III
(for chapter two)

> . . . God did not spare angels when they sinned, but cast them into hell [Gr. Tartarus—Compartment in Sheol] and committed them to pits of darkness, reserved for judgment; and did not spare the ancient world, but preserved Noah, a preacher of righteousness, with seven others, when He brought a flood upon the world of the ungodly (II Pet. 2:4-5).

Bible Synopsis of "deep" (Heb. $t^e hom$)

And the earth was formless and void, and darkness was over the surface of the deep; and the spirit of God was moving over the surface of the waters (Gen. 1:2).

$T^e hom$, "deep," occurs thirty-five times in the Old Testament. It means the subterranean springs under the Earth (Deut. 8:7), the lowest depths of the oceans (Job 38:16-17) and the lowest depths of the Earth.

The lowest depths of the oceans is by far the most common usage. The two areas of the lowest depths are the Puerto Rican Trench, 27,500 feet at the bottom of the Bermuda Triangle and the Mariana Trench, 36,198 feet just south of the Devil's Sea off the coast of Japan.

A study of the word "deep" in conjunction with the nether world shows the following correlations:

1. The subterranean depths of the sea are the *entrances* into the nether world for Sheol-Hades.

"Have you entered into the springs of the sea? Or have you walked in the recesses of the deep? Have the gates of death been revealed to you? Or have you seen the gates of deep darkness?" (Job 38:16-17).

2. These depths act as bars to a prison.

"Water becomes hard like stone, and the surface of the deep is imprisoned" (Job 38:30).

"Water encompassed me to the *very* soul, the great deep engulfed me. . . . The earth with its bars was around me forever, but Thou hast brought up my life from the pit, O LORD my God" (Jonah 2:5-6).

3. Leviathan, the sea monster of pride, causes these depths to boil like a pot.

"Can you draw out Leviathan with a fish-hook? . . . he makes the depths boil like a pot; he makes the sea like a jar of ointment" (Job 41:1, 31).

"Praise the LORD from the earth, sea monsters and all deeps" (Psa. 148:7).

Egypt's earthly symbol of the beast is a crocodile, a sea serpent, a dragon called Rahab who was cut into pieces at the deliverance of Israel from Pharaoh. The depths of the Red Sea were rolled back and then closed again covering Pharaoh and his army (Isa. 51:9-11; 63:12-13). Leviathan is discussed fully in Chapter 7.

4. Depths symbolize troubles and distresses.

"Thou, who hast shown me many troubles and distresses, wilt revive me again, and wilt bring me up again from the depths of the earth" (Psa. 71:20).

The analogy here, according to some translators, is that the "earth" is the Sheol-Hades compartment. The Rich Man in Sheol-Hades had distress:

    a.   He was in torment (Luke 16:23, 28).

    b.   He wanted his tongue to be cooled (Luke 16:24).

    c.   He was in agony in a flame (Luke 16:24-25).
        Amos the Prophet says concerning Israel in conjunction with flame-depths

        ". . . the Lord GOD was calling to contend with them (Israel) by fire, and it consumed the great deep and began to consume the farm land" (Amos 7:4).

    d.   He had a concern for the lost (too late)—(Luke 16:27-31).

5.   The deep is a storehouse.

"He gathers the waters of the sea together as a heap; He lays up the deeps in storehouses" (Psa. 33:7).

Here deeps is in conjunction with God's creation. He puts them in storehouses, reserved for harvest. Could this be the storehouse awaiting God's judgment in the end time, when He will roll back the curtain of the depths and let all men look into the Sheol-Hades entrance? Isaiah implies this:

"Thy judgments are like a great deep" (Psa. 36:6).

This is in contrast to the righteousness of God which is like a mountain.

6.   Depths associated with the compartment of Sheol-Hades in judgment.

    a.   Christ's judgment for our sins

"I called out of my distress to the LORD, and He answered me. I cried for help from the depth of Sheol; Thou didst hear my voice" (Jonah 2:2).

"For just as Jonah was there three days and three nights in the belly of the sea monster, so shall the Son of Man be three days and three nights in the heart of the earth" (Matt. 12:40). (See I Pet. 3:19).

b. Noahic judgment

". . . all the fountains of the great deep burst open, and the floodgates of the sky were opened" (Gen. 7:11).

"Also the fountains of the deep and the floodgates of the sky were closed, and the rain from the sky was restrained" (Gen. 8:2).

"By His knowledge the deeps were broken up, and the skies drip with dew" (Prov. 3:20).

c. Luciferian judgment

"And the earth was formless and void, and darkness was over the surface of the deep; and the Spirit of God was moving over the surface of the waters" (Gen. 1:2).

"Thou didst cover it with the deep as with a garment; the waters were standing above the mountains. At Thy rebuke they fled" (Psa. 104:5-9).

d. Tyre judgment

"For thus says the Lord GOD, 'When I shall

make you a desolate city, like the cities which are not inhabited, when I shall bring up the deep over you, and the great waters will cover you, then I shall bring you down with those who go down in the lower parts of the earth, . . . with those who go down to the pit' . . ." (Ezek. 26:19-20).

e. Assyria and Egypt judgment

"Thus says the Lord GOD, 'On the day when it went down to Sheol I caused lamentations; I closed the deep over it and held back its rivers . . . I made the nations quake at the sound of its fall when I made it go down to Sheol with those who go down to the pit . . .' " (Ezek. 31:15-16).

7. The *depths* have voices and call to other *depths* through sea-going tornadoes.

"Deep calleth unto deep at the noise of thy waterspouts: all Thy waves and Thy billows are gone over me" (Psa. 42:7 KJV).

"The mountains saw Thee *and* quaked; the downpour of waters swept by. The deep uttered forth its voice, it lifted high its hands" (Hab. 3:10).

For this they willingly are ignorant of, that by the word of God the heavens were of old, and the earth standing out of the water and in the water: Whereby the world that then was, being overflowed with water, perished: But the heavens and the earth, which are now, by the same word are kept in store, reserved unto fire against the day of judgment and perdition of ungodly men (II Pet. 3:5-7 KJV).

Reasons for this section referring to the Luciferian Flood:

1. The "out of water and in the water" refers to the *condition* of the Earth in Gen. 1:6-10.

    a. The Earth was in a flooded state. In the original Greek, the phrase "in the water" means a condition or state.*

2. The Earth was being "placed together."

    a. The Greek word for "standing" means "to place together." This same word in Colossians is translated "hold together," speaking of Christ's power in creation.

    > ". . . all things have been created through Him and for Him. And he is before all things, and in Him all things hold together" (Col. 1:16-17).

    b. In II Pet. 3:5, in the original Greek word order, "hold together" should go with the phrase "by the word of God," not with "out of the water and in the water." It should read like this:

    > "For this they willingly are ignorant of, that the heavens were of old and the earth out of the water and in the water was placed together by the word of God . . ." (II Pet. 3:5).

---

* Robertson, Archibald T., *Word Pictures in the New Testament* (Broadman Press, Nashville, Tenn., 1933) vol. VI, p. 174, verse 5.

This would correspond with:

(1). Col. 1:16-17
    That Christ the living word spoke into the existence the re-creation of Genesis 1. The words "God said," occur seven times in the renovation of the Earth.

(2). Gen. 1:9
    "Then God said, 'Let the waters below and heavens be gathered into one place, and let the dry land appear;' and it was so."

This wording agrees with II Pet. 3:5, "gathered together."

Almost every Bible scholar agrees that II Pet. 3:5 refers to the water of Genesis 1, though many of them say it was the "water" of the original creation process, not the water of judgment of the Luciferian Flood. Coming to II Pet. 3:6, these same scholars say that this now is the Noahic Flood.*

3. II Pet. 3:6 cannot be the Noahic Flood but agrees with II Pet. 3:5 being the destructive flood of the fall of Lucifer.

    a. The first word of II Pet. 3:6 is "whereby," which in the original Greek is a phrase meaning "by which means." † This was by the means of water in the Luciferian judgment. It would read like this:

---

* Whitcomb, John C. Jr., and Morris, John C., *The Genesis Flood* (Baker Book House, Grand Rapids, Mich., 1961), pp. 16, 214, 215, 228-232.
† Robertson, *loc. cit.*

"For this they willingly are ignorant of, that by the word of God the heavens were of old, and the earth standing out of the water and in the water: whereby (by which means) the world that then was overflowed with water, perished" (II Pet. 3:5-6).

b. The phrase "the world that then was" refers to the world of II Pet. 3:5. If the "then world" refers to the Noahic Flood, it would confuse the reader to have jumped thousands of years from Genesis 1 to Genesis 8 between II Pet. 3:5 and 3:6.

Also, the "then world" is contrasted with the "heavens and the earth," which "are now" in II Pet. 3:7.

c. The word for "world" in II Pet. 3:6 is *kosmos*, meaning "a social order" in the pre-Luciferian Flood age and agrees with Jer. 4:23-26.

4. Three theologians agree that water in Genesis 1 is the Luciferian Flood of judgment.

a. J. Sidlow Baxter, *Explore the Book*, vol. 1, p. 42.

b. Kenneth Wuest, *In These Last Days*, p. 67.

c. Finis Dake, *Annotated Bible*, p. 1, Gen. 1:1.

IV
(for chapter six)

Other places where the Hebrew word *bor* is used with "Sheol:"

1. O Lord, Thou hast brought up my soul from Sheol;
   Thou hast kept me alive, that I should not go down
   to the pit (Psa. 30:3).

2. And my life has drawn near to Sheol. I am reckoned
   among those who go down to the pit; . . .

   Thou hast put me in the lowest pit, In dark places,
   in the depths (Psa. 88:3, 4, 6).

In this section we have "depths;" subterranean waters are connected with the "pit" and "Sheol." Also, verse 88:11 is "destruction—Abaddon;" the King of the abyss is mentioned (Rev. 9:11).

3. Let us swallow them alive like Sheol, Even whole,
   as those who go down to the pit . . . (Prov. 1:12).

Other Hebrew words for "pit," "cistern," "well," are: *Be'er*—(Psa. 55:23), *Gebe*—(Isa. 30:14), *Guwmmats*—(Ecc. 10:8), *Pachath*—(II Sam. 17:9), *Shiychah*—(Prov. 22:14), *Shachath*—used with "Sheol" (Job 17:14; Psa. 9:15, 16:10, 30:9, 49:9, 55:23, 94:13, Isa. 38:17; Jonah 2:6).

Shachath is the word for "pit"—a concealed, hidden trap in the ground to catch animals.

Cave of Machpelah

The first mention in the Bible of a family burial plot was Abraham's cave at Machpelah.

In Genesis 23, following the death of Sarah, his wife,

Abraham, being a stranger in the land of Canaan, requested from its citizens a plot to bury his wife. The sons of Heth replied, "Hear us, my lord, you are a mighty prince among us; bury your dead in the choicest of our graves" (Gen. 23:6).

Then Abraham requested the choicest funeral plot—the cave of Machpelah, which was owned by Ephron, a wealthy citizen of the land. Ephron refused Abraham's money, offering to give it to him as a gift. However, Abraham insisted that he take four hundred shekels of silver, "so the field and the cave that is in it, were deeded over to Abraham for a burial site by the sons of Heth" (Gen. 23:20).

Later Abraham also was buried there (Gen. 25:9). And Isaac "was gathered to his people" (Gen. 35:29).

Jacob refused to be buried in Egypt and charged his sons to take his bones back to the cave of Machpelah (Gen. 49:29-33). He was embalmed by the Egyptians and in a great funeral processional, Joseph and his brothers took him from Egypt to Canaan (Gen. 50:26).

Some years later, Joseph's body was also carried to the cave of Machpelah. This was done when Moses led the children of Israel in Exodus from Egypt (Exo. 13:19).

"Sheol" is mentioned for the first time during the life of Jacob (Gen. 37:35, 42:38, 44:29, 31). There was a special significance to *where* they were buried.

They didn't want their bodies placed in Egyptian tombs with their polytheistic gods but with Abraham who is the father of all true believers.

Hence the correlation of a believer's funeral plot for the body and a place in the nether world for the spirit and soul. There was a double compartment in Luke 16:22-28 for the righteous and unrighteous.

V
(for chapter seven)

There are four words that are translated "sea monster," "dragon" and "sea serpent" in the Old Testament. One of these, *tan*,—jackel—is wrongly translated "dragon" in fourteen places in the King James Version of the Old Testament. The New American Standard (NAS) correctly translates "jackel" in thirteen places and "night monster" in one.

Leviathan occurs five times and is translated by that name on all five occurrences.

Leviathan—(Heb. *liv-yah-thahn'*)—five occurrences:

1. Let those curse it who curse the day, Who are prepared to rouse Leviathan (Job 3:8).

Job is speaking of the *night* in which he was born, Job 3:6-7—may they curse it as well as the day of his birth. This is all said in the light of his trials as he heaps ridicule upon his suffering self.

The problem of "the one who curses the night" is likened to the difficulty of one who tries to rouse Leviathan from the deep dark waters of the seas. It is easier to curse the *day* of Job's birth, because one can see the characteristics of it, than it is to *curse the night* or *rouse Leviathan,* because you cannot see the night nor Leviathan who is hiding in the deep.

2. Can you draw out Leviathan with a fish-hook? Or press down his tongue with a cord? (Job 41:1).

The forty-first chapter deals with the sea monster. The last verse depicts him as "the king over all the sons of pride." Leviathan becomes the personification of Satan with the spiritual form of a serpentine sea monster.

199

3. Thou didst crush the heads of Leviathan; thou didst give him as food for the creatures of the wilderness (Psa. 74:14).

The Psalmist is speaking of Egypt during the Exodus. The sea monster in verse 13 is the Hebrew *tannin*, a symbol of Egypt, possibly the crocodile. When Pharaoh and all his hosts drowned, so was their crocodile sea god destroyed. Leviathan is symbolic of the might of Satan who was crushed by the power of God in Israel's deliverance and supernatural provision in the wilderness. On the one hand, God feeds them "angel's food" and sustains them for forty years, and on the other hand, He feeds the fears and taunts of Leviathan to the creatures of the Sinai Desert.

It was Moses' rod that became a serpent (Heb. *tanneen'*—sea serpent, possibly a crocodile), that ate up the Egyptians' rods which also became sea serpents (Exod. 7:10-12).

4. There is the sea, great and broad, in which are swarms without number, animals both small and great and Leviathan, which Thou hast formed to sport in it (Psa. 104:25-26).

The Psalmist makes reference to a creature of the sea that was well known to the Hebrew minds of their day.

5. In that day the LORD will punish Leviathan the fleeing serpent, with His fierce and great and mighty sword, even Leviathan the twisted serpent; who *lives* in the sea (Isa. 27:1).

The dragon is Satan in Rev. 12:3. John saw "a great red dragon," which most commentators say is the devil as mentioned in Rev. 20:2, also called *serpent of old* and Satan. The Hebrew word for "dragon" in Isa. 27:1 is *tan-neen'*—sea serpent. Both Leviathan and dragon in this passage stand for a large marine animal, not a land serpent (Heb. *nachish*).

Dragon—(Heb. *tan-neen'*)—sea serpent, monster:

Refers to any large marine creature. In Gen. 1:21, "the great sea monsters" could refer to any of the ancient plesiosaurs, sea-reptiles and large primitive whales—now extinct.

Pharaoh's magicians threw their rods on the ground, and they became serpents—possibly crocodiles from the Nile River, one of the Egyptian deities. It was this evil sea serpent called Rahab in Isa. 51:9 and Leviathan in Psa. 74:14 that was "crushed, cut up and fed to the creatures of the wilderness," symbolic of God destroying the might of Egypt in the Red Sea and conquering their sea god.

Fourteen occurrences:

1. And God created the great sea monsters . . . (Gen. 1:21).

2. Take your staff and throw *it* down before Pharaoh, *that* it may become a serpent (Exod. 7:9).

3. And Aaron threw his staff down before Pharaoh and it became a serpent (Exod. 7:10).

4. For each one [Pharaoh's magicians] threw down his staff and they turned into serpents. But Aaron's staff swallowed up their staffs (Exod. 7:12).

5. Their wine is the venom of serpents, and the deadly poison of cobras (Deut. 32:33).

6. So I [Nehemiah] went out at night by the Valley Gate in the direction of the Dragon's Well and on to the Refuse Gate, inspecting the walls of Jerusalem (Neh. 2:13).

7. Am I [Job] the sea, or the sea monster, that Thou dost set a guard over me? (Job 7:12).

Note: Sheol is used in this section (verse 9).

When a cloud vanishes, it is gone, so he who goes down to Sheol does not come up. He will not return again to his house, nor will his place know him any more (Job 7:9-10).

8. Thou didst divide the sea by Thy strength; Thou didst break the heads of the sea monsters in the waters. Thou didst crush the heads of Leviathan. Thou didst give him as food for the creatures of the wilderness (Psa. 74:13, 14).

9. You will tread upon the lion and cobra, the young lion and the serpent you will trample down (Psa. 91:13).

Note: Here "deeps" are connected with *sea monsters*.

10. Praise the LORD from the earth, sea-monsters and all deeps (Psa. 148:7).

11. In that day the LORD will punish Leviathan the fleeing serpent, with His fierce and great and mighty sword, even Leviathan the twisted serpent; and He will kill the dragon who lives in the sea (Isa. 27:1).

12. Awake, awake put on strength, O arm of the LORD; awake as in the days of old the generations of long long ago. Was it not Thou who cut Rahab in pieces, who pierced the dragon? (Isa. 51:9).

Note: Here the name of Rahab refers to this sea monster as in Job 9:13, 26:12; Psa. 89:10.*

---

* Brown, Francis; Driver, S.R.; Briggs, C.A., *Lexicon* p. 923, Heb. *Rahab*.

13. Nebuchadnezzar, king of Babylon, has devoured me and crushed me, he has set me down like an empty vessel; he has swallowed me like a monster, he has filled his stomach with my delicacies; he has washed me away (Jer. 51:34).

14. Son of man, take up a lamentation over Pharaoh king of Egypt, and say to him, "you compared yourself to a young lion of the nations, Yet you are like the monster in the seas; And you burst forth in your rivers, and muddied the waters with your feet, and fouled their rivers" (Ezek. 32:2).

Rahab—(Heb. *ra'-hab*), sea serpent, Egyptian deity: Rahab, according to Brown, Driver and Briggs, is an ancient Hebrew mythical sea serpent. Job records him twice, while in Psalms Rahab refers to an Egyptian deity who was crushed in the Red Sea.

1. God will not turn back His anger; Beneath Him crouch the helpers of Rahab (Job 9:13).

Could the *helpers of Rahab* refer to demon personages under the control of this evil power of the seas?

2. He quieted the sea with His power, and by His understanding He shattered Rahab. By His breath the heavens are cleared; His hand has pierced the fleeing serpent [Heb. *nachish*—land serpent] (Job 26:12-13).

Here Rahab is connected with the sea, and by God's understanding Rahab was shattered. In the next verse the word for land serpent further describes this serpentine sea monster—"the fleeing serpent."

3. Thou dost rule the swelling of the sea; When its waves rise, Thou dost still them. Thou Thyself didst crush Rahab like one who is slain; Thou didst scatter Thine enemies with Thy mighty arm (Psa. 89:9-10).

Here Rahab is again connected with the "swelling of the sea" and rising of the waves. It is God who crushes this sea serpent, His ancient enemy.

VI
(for chapter eight)

Abaddon: "In NT found only in Rev. 9:11. The name of an angel of the underworld, of the king of the Scorpion-Centaurs who will plague men in the last days. The name is rendered Apolluon 'the Destroyer' in Greek. It is part of the cryptic style of the Apocalyptist to use the Hebrew name in the Greek text.

"The name is taken from the OT. In Job 26:6, 28:22; Prov. 15:11, and Psa. 88:12 from the Hebrew . . . the 'place of destruction,' and to describe the world of the dead. The personification as speakers, has given rise to the notion of an angel of Hell who in Rev. 9:11 is identified with the prince of the underworld." *

Seven Heads

In the book of Revelation, the term "seven heads" is used three times. All are symbolic of the seven world empires that have been in possession of Palestine. The three symbols are:

1. Dragon having seven heads—Rev. 12:3. Symbolic of the devil.
2. Beast coming up out of the sea having seven heads—Rev. 13:1. Symbolic of Antichrist.
3. Woman sitting on a scarlet beast having seven heads—Rev. 17:3. Symbolic of the prostitute religions of the world.

These seven heads all refer to the same thing—nations that have controlled Israel during the "times of the Gentiles"

---

* Kittel, *op. cit.*, vol. I, p. 4, (Joachim Jeremias).

(Luke 21:24). The seven nations, which have and will dominate Israel until the coming of Christ, are:

1. Egypt—symbol is a crocodile sea serpent (Rahab)—possessed Israel for four hundred years until the deliverance of Moses.
2. Assyria—symbol is a lion—ruled Israel for more than four hundred years, on and off.
3. Babylon—symbol is an eagle—ruled Israel for more than two hundred years.
4. Medes and Persians—Symbol is a bear—ruled over Israel for more than one hundred years.
5. Greece—symbol is a leopard—ruled Israel for more than two hundred years.
6. Rome—symbol is a nondescript beast—ruled over Israel for close to one thousand years.
7. Revised Rome—symbol still nondescript beast—will rule over Israel for the first three-and-a-half years of the tribulation period when the Antichrist will consolidate the ten countries in the geographical region of the old Roman Empire. These are the ten horns spoken of in these symbols.

The eighth and final kingdom will be the one over which Antichrist will personally rule during the last three-and-one-half years of the Tribulation. This kingdom will end in the battle of Armageddon, after which Christ will set up His one thousand year rule.*

---

* Dake, *op. cit.*, p. 311, col. 1, 2.

Notes
Chapter 1

[1] Whitcomb, John C. Jr., and Morris, Henry, *The Genesis Flood* (Baker Book House, Grand Rapids, Mich., 1961), p. 178.

[2] *Ibid.*, p. 179. See also "The Chambered Nautilus," January 1976, pp. 38-41, *National Geographic.*

[3] *The Daily Breeze*, Torrance, Calif., March 26, 1974.

[4] *National Tattler*, July 6, 1975, p. 36.

Authors' note: Since this article appeared in the *National Tattler*, we have spoken to Wayne Meshejian at Longwood College in Farmville, Va., where he was teaching a class in physics. He took time out to explain to us the controversy over the NOAA satellites. He questions the reliability of the government's explanation about the blackouts. He says government officials have changed their story about the reason for the blackouts several times. He still believes the government is withholding some information.

[5] Berlitz, Charles, *The Bermuda Triangle* (Doubleday & Company Inc., Garden City, N.Y., 1974), p. 127.

[6] *Ibid.*, p. 165.

[7] Villiers, Alan, *Wild Ocean*, 1957.

[8] *Midnight*, June 16, 1975.

Authors' note: Since this incident, which happened on Feb. 21, 1975, we have talked with Betty Miller. She not only confirmed this story, but testified that she is a charismatic Catholic and loves Jesus Christ. She and her husband operate a 400-acre radish farm in East Lansing, Michigan. During the winter months, they do missionary work in Guatemala.

[9] Berlitz, *op. cit.*, p. 112.

[10] *Ibid.*, pp. 119-120.

[11] *Ibid.*, pp. 119-120.

[12] *Ibid.*, pp. 116-117.

[13] *Ibid.*, p. 102.

[14] *Ibid.*, pp. 20-21.

[15] Weldon, John, *UFOs: What On Earth Is Happening?* (Harvest House Publishers, Irvine, Calif., 1975), pp. 120-121.

[16] *Ibid.*

[17] *Ibid.*, p. 3.

[18] Chafer, Lewis S., *Systematic Theology* (Dallas: Seminary Press, 1971), vol. I, p. 117.

[19] Jeffrey, Adi-Kent Thomas, *The Bermuda Triangle* (Warner Paperback Library, P.O. Box 690, N.Y., N.Y. 10019, 1975), p. 174.

[20] Berlitz, *op. cit.*, pp. 205-206.

[21] *National Tattler*, Jan. 26, 1975.

Notes
Chapter 2

[1] Whitcomb, John C., Jr., & Morris, Henry M., *The Genesis Flood* (Baker Book House, Grand Rapids, Mich., 1961), pp. 219-221.

[2] *Ibid.*, pp. 137-139.

[3] *Ibid.*, p. 126.

[4] Fenneman, N.M., *Physiography of Western United States* (New York, N.Y., McGraw-Hill, 1931), p. 11.

[5] Whitcomb & Morris, *op. cit.*, p. 153.

[6] Velikovsky, I., *Earth in Upheaval* (Doubleday & Company, N.Y., 1955), p. 22.

[7] Brogersma, M., & Sanders, "Treatise on Marine Ecology and Paleoecology," vol. I, *Geological Society of America Memoir* 67, 1957, p. 972.

[8] *Ibid.*, pp. 154-165.

[9] Lyell, Charles, *Principles of Geology* (11th ed., rev., New York, D. Appleton & Co., 1892), vol. I, pp. 317-318.

[10] Darwin, Charles, *The Origin of Species by Means of Natural Selection*, vol. XLIX of Great Books of the Western World, ed. Robert M. Hutchins (Chicago: Encyclopedia Britannica Inc., 1952), p. 153.

[11] Haber, Francis H., *The Age of the World: Moses to Darwin* (The Johns Hopkins Press, Baltimore, Maryland, 1959), p. 153.

[12] Robinson, Lytle W., *Edgar Cayce's Story of the Origin and Destiny of Man* (Coward, McCann & Geoghegan Inc., N.Y., 1972), pp. 40-51.

[13] Jeffrey, Adi-Kent Thomas, *The Bermuda Triangle* (Warner Paperback Library, P.O. Box 690, N.Y., N.Y., 10019, 1975), p. 187.

[14] Robinson, *op. cit.*, pp. 9-11.

[15] Berlitz, Charles, *The Bermuda Triangle* (Avon Books, 959 Eighth Avenue, N.Y., N.Y., 1974), p. 171.

[16] Von Daniken, Erich, *Gods From Outer Space* (Bantam Books, G.P. Putnam's Sons, 200 Madison Avenue, N.Y., N.Y., 10016, 1971), p. 141.

[17] Cerve, W.S., *Lemuria* (Kings Port Press Inc., Kingsport, Tenn., 8th ed., 1960), chapters V-XI.

[18] Baldwin, John Denison, *Prehistoric Nations* (London & N.Y., 1869), pp. 148, 155.

[19] Donnelly, Ignatius, *The Antediluvian World* (Harper & Brothers, Gramercy Pub. Co., Rev. Ed., 1949 by Edgerton Sykes), p. 22.

[20] Schott, Arthur, "Smithsonian Reports," 1869, p. 391.

Notes
Chapter 3

[1] Some of the smoke probably was laid down by the English navy, and combined with the battle smoke that was blown out to sea, became an answer to prayer, thus providing a supernatural cover for the escaping British army.

[2] Taylor, A.J.P., *Purnell's History of the 20th Century* (Purnell, 850 7th Avenue, New York, N.Y., 1971), vol. 7, pp. 1707-1708.

[3] Berlitz, Charles, *The Bermuda Triangle* (Avon Books, 959 Eighth Avenue, N.Y., N.Y., 1974), p. 58.

[4] Deut. 17:16.

[5] Josh. 11:4-9.

[6] Berlitz, *loc. cit.*

Notes
Chapter 4

[1] Also called Bermuda Triangle. The Devil's Triangle and Bermuda Triangle are used interchangeably in this text. The Bermuda Triangle is so named because one of its apexes touches Bermuda.

[2] Some writers pinpoint the Florida apex at Miami rather than extend it into the Gulf of Mexico.

[3] *Los Angeles Times*, "FAA Not Mystified By Bermuda Triangle," Nov. 10, 1975.

[4] *Ibid.*

[5] Winer, Richard, *The Devil's Triangle 2* (Bantam Books Inc., New York, N.Y., 1975), pp. 13-14.

[6] Kusche, Lawrence David, *The Bermuda Triangle Mystery—Solved* (Harper & Row, New York, N.Y., 1975), p. 277.

[7] *Ibid.*, p. 275.

[8] Kusche is a reference librarian at Arizona State University with commercial and instructor pilot's rating. He did research by collecting all the corresponding news, government and research committees' reports in the same years and months of the disappearances.

[9] Kusche, *op. cit.*, p. 276.

[10] Rom. 1:18-28.

[11] Kusche, *op. cit.*, pp. 159-160.

[12] *Ibid.*, pp. 230-231.

[13] Stewart-Gordon, James, "What's the Truth About the Bermuda Triangle?" *The Reader's Digest*, July 1975.

[14] Kusche, *op. cit.*, p. 184.

[15] *Ibid.*, pp. 200-204.

[16] Stewart-Gordon, *loc. cit.*

[17] Kusche, *op. cit.*, p. 100.

[18] *Ibid.*, p. 104.

[19] *Ibid.*, p. 116.

[20] Stewart-Gordon, *loc. cit.*

[21] *Miami Herald*, Sunday, March 7, 1948, p. 1, col. 4; and Monday, March 8, 1948, p. B1.

[22] Kusche, *op. cit.*, pp. 170-171.

[23] Berlitz, Charles, *The Bermuda Triangle* (Doubleday & Company Inc., Garden City, N.Y., 1974), pp. 66-67.

[24] *Miami Herald*, Tuesday, June 8, 1965, p. 12. See also June 7 edition.

[25] Kusche, *op. cit.*, p. 210.

[26] *Midnight*, Oct. 15, 1973, p. 11; Oct. 22, p. 11; Oct. 29, p. 7.

[27] Psa. 135:5-7.

[28] I Kings 19:11-12.

[29] King of the sea. Leviathan is discussed in chapter 7.

[30] See their story in chapter 1.

Notes
Chapter 5

[1] Sheol is mentioned sixty-five times in the Old Testament. King James Version translators translated it as "grave" in thirty-two references. The New American Standard version invariably transliterates Sheol, as do several other modern translations. All sixty-five references concern the abode of departed spirits in the nether world.

[2] Gen. 6:1-4; I Pet. 3:19, 20; Jude 6.

[3] Diabolical ruler of endtime who Bible prophecy students believe will control Western Europe and the world's free nations for seven years before Armageddon.

[4] Some Bible scholars say the word "sea" represents "nations," basing their interpretations on Rev. 17:15 (waters are "peoples, and multitudes, and nations, and tongues"). While their interpretation of this passage is correct, it cannot be applied to the word "sea" in Rev. 13:1. "Sea" in this passage is *thalasse.* "Waters" in Rev. 17:15 is *hudor.* We take "sea" literally because the Sheol-Hades compartment is under the sea and because "waters" in Rev. 17:15 and "sea" in Rev. 13:1 are two different Greek words.

[5] Fox, Lorne F., *Visions of Heaven, Hell and the Cross* (Privately published, P.O. Box 34, Naselle, Wash.), pp. 15-20.

[6] Lindsay, Gordon, ed., *Scenes Beyond the Grave* (Christ For The Nations, Dallas, Tex., 1973), pp. 61-73.

[7] Bergier, Jacques, *Secret Doors of the Earth* (Henry Regnery Co., 180 North Michigan Ave., Chicago, Ill., 1975), pp. 22, 23.

[8] *Ibid.*, p. 51.

[9] *Ibid.*, p. 52.

Notes
Chapter 6

[1] Life Reprint, "Scientists Close in on the Secret of Life," 1963, *Time* Inc. (Rockefeller Center, N.Y., N.Y.).
This article shows how these tiny building blocks have four pre-recorded chemical messages that govern all life on this planet (Adenine, Thymine, Guanine and Cytosine). Isn't it interesting that in the creation of Genesis 1, God "spoke" into existence each species of life after his kind. All life was pre-recorded on DNA tapes by God Himself! The Divine "song" goes on by the fantastic reproduction of "His tapes," "for by Him all things are *held together*" (Col. 1:17). Also, "For since the creation of the world His invisible attributes, His eternal power and divine nature, have been so clearly seen, *being understood through what has been made,* so that they are without excuse" (Rom. 1:20).

[2] Revelle, Roger, "The Ocean," *Scientific American,* September 1969, p. 64.

[3] *Ibid.,* p. 65.

[4] Kittel, Gerhard, *Theological Dictionary of the New Testament* (Wm. B. Eerdmans Publishing Company, Grand Rapids, Mich., 1964), vol. I, p. 146.

[5] Dake, Finis Jennings, *Dake's Annotated Reference Bible* (Dake Bible Sales Inc., P.O. Box 173, Lawrenceville, Ga. 30245), p. 537, col. 1, note e.

[6] Olson, Nathanael, "How Deep Is the Ocean," *The Pentecostal Evangel,* Oct. 28, 1956.

[7] Dake, *op. cit.,* p. 272.

[8] Pardington, George P., *Outline Studies in Christian Doctrine* (Christian Publications Inc., 25 South Tenth Street, Harrisburg, Pa.), p. 122, "Origin."

[9] Berlitz, *op. cit.,* pp. 94-95.

Notes
Chapter 7

[1] Winer, Richard, *The Devil's Triangle* (Bantam Books Inc., 666 Fifth Ave., N.Y., N.Y., 1974), pp. 202-203.

[2] Berlitz, *op. cit.,* pp. 4-5.

[3] *Ibid.,* p. 5.

[4] *Ibid.,* p. 4.

[5] Costello, Peter, *In Search of Lake Monsters* (Coward, McCann Geoghegan Inc., 200 Madison Ave., N.Y., N.Y., 1974), pp. 315-316.

[6] *Ibid.,* p. 316.

[7] *Ibid.,* p. 316.

[8] Gunther, Marty, "New Sighting of Loch Ness Monster!" *The National Tattler*, Aug. 7, 1975.

[9] "The Case for the Loch Ness Monster," *Science News*, April 17, 1976, p. 247.

[10] "Loch Ness Search Sponsored by Times," *Ibid.*, June 5 & 12, 1976, p. 359.

[11] Costello, *op. cit.*, p. 25.

[12] *Ibid.*, p. 26.

[13] *Ibid.*, p. 132.

[14] *Ibid.*, p. 154.

[15] *Ibid.*, p. 155.

[16] *Ibid.*, p. 181.

[17] *Ibid.*, p. 207.

[18] *Ibid.*, p. 217.

[19] *Ibid.*, p. 305.

[20] *Ibid.*, p. 305.

[21] Berlitz, *op. cit.*, p. 60.

[22] *Ibid.*, p. 67.

[23] Pember, G.H., *Earth's Earliest Ages* (Fleming H. Revell Co., Old Tappan, N.J.), pp. 225-228.

Notes
Chapter 8

[1] Dake, *op. cit.*, second page of the Preface.

[2] Kittel, *op. cit.*, vol. I, p. 4, article by Joachim Jeremias.

Notes
Chapter 9

[1] Psa. 9:17. See also Prov. 9:18.

[2] Job 26:5.

[3] II Pet. 2:4.

[4] Luke 8:30-33.

[5] I Pet. 3:19.

[6] Compiled by John Myers; published by Pyramid Books, New York, N.Y., 1968.

[7] Fox, *Visions of Heaven, Hell and the Cross*, pp. 19, 20.

[8] Lindsay, *Scenes Beyond the Grave*, pp. 61, 62.

[9] *Ibid.*, pp. 64-67.

[10] *Ibid.*, pp. 68-81.

[11] Baker, H.A., *Visions Beyond the Veil* (Whitaker Books, Monroeville, Penn., 1973), pp. 88, 89.

[12] Hagen, Kenneth, *I Believe in Visions* (Fleming H. Revell Co., Old Tappan, N.J., 1972), pp. 44.

Notes
Chapter 10

[1] "Lung disease from the ocean," *Science News*, May 29, 1976.
[2] "Cousteau says sea is dying," *Los Angeles Times*, Nov. 1, 1975.
[3] Other passages on the millennial reign of Christ are Zechariah 14; Isa. 65:18-25; Isa. 66:18-21, and Ezekiel 38 through 48.
[4] Dake, p. 730.